Writing Poetry to Save Your Life

Writing Poetry to Save Your Life:

How to Find the Courage to Tell Your Stories

Maria Mazziotti Gillan

MiroLand
publishers

MIROLAND (GUERNICA)

TORONTO – BUFFALO – BERKELEY – LANCASTER (U.K.) 2013

Michael Mirolla, general editor
Connie McParland, editor
Guernica Editions Inc.
P.O. Box 117, Station P, Toronto (ON), Canada M5S 2S6
2250 Military Road, Tonawanda, N.Y. 14150-6000 U.S.A.

Distributors:
University of Toronto Press Distribution,
5201 Dufferin Street, Toronto (ON), Canada M3H 5T8
Gazelle Book Services, White Cross Mills, High
Town, Lancaster LA1 4XS U.K.
Small Press Distribution, 1341 Seventh St., Berkeley, CA 94710-1409 U.S.A.

First edition.

Legal Deposit – First Quarter

Library of Congress Catalog Card Number: 2012952522

Library and Archives Canada Cataloguing in Publication

Gillan, Maria M.
Writing poetry to save your life : how to find the courage
to tell your stories / Maria Mazziotti Gillan.
Also issued in electronic format.
ISBN 978-1-55071-747-1
1. Poetry--Authorship. I. Title.
PN1059.A9G54 2013   808.1   C2012-907315-6

Contents

Part Four: Learning Courage

Introduction

When I first started to consider putting together a book about writing poetry, I thought about how frightened people often are by the idea of poetry – writing it, reading it, feeling that they have anything to write about that anyone else would be interested in reading. I realized that my whole life as a poet and teacher was dedicated to giving people a feeling that their lives, that what they have to say, is important.

I believe we all have stories to tell, and that those stories are the basis for writing poems that reach across the barriers of age, ethnicity, gender, social class to connect with all that is human inside us. I think of William Faulkner's Nobel Prize acceptance speech in which he said: "Writing today has forgotten the problems of the human heart in conflict with itself which alone can make good writing because only that is worth writing about, worth the agony and the sweat."

In order to overcome our own fear about writing, our own lack of self-confidence in facing the blank page, we need to learn to let go. When we're writing, we need to get to that place where the pen moves almost by itself.

What I hope to accomplish in this book is to give writing prompts that will help you to get past all the outside influences that keep you from believing in yourself and in your ability to write. In order to write, you need to get rid of notions about language, poetic form, and esoteric subject matter – all the things that the poetry police have told you are essential if you are to write. I wanted to start from a different place, a place controlled by instinct rather than by intelligence. Revision, the shaping and honing of the poem, should come later, and, in revising, be careful to retain the vitality and electricity of the poem. Anyone can learn to craft a capable poem, but it is the poems that retain that initial vitality that we remember; these are the poems that teach us how to be human.

When I first started to write, I read an enormous amount of poetry and was influenced by that poetry to imitate these famous poets. Those years of imitation taught me about the beauty of language, the music of it, the way that words shaped into a poem can sing as the poems of Dylan Thomas sing. Gradually, I discovered a very American music in the poems of Walt Whitman and Allen Ginsberg. "The universal is in the particular," William Carlos Williams said, and he influenced American poets from Ginsberg to Galway Kinnell to Lucille Clifton to Sharon Olds to Jimmy Santiago Baca to Mark Doty to Anne Sexton to Adrienne Rich to Stanley Kunitz to Robert Creeley. Under the influence of Whitman and Williams and Ginsberg, American poets have generated an impressive body of electric, exciting, original, and moving *American* writing.

Since I started out imitating Keats and Shelley, I was 40 before I learned to believe that people might be interested in reading poetry by a working-class Italian American mother, wife, and grandmother from Paterson, New Jersey. It was a professor in graduate school who gave me the courage to believe in my own story. It is this courage I try to impart to my students – whether they are the graduate and undergraduate students at Binghamton University, State University of New York; the writers attending the many intensive workshops that I have conducted with poet Laura Boss; or the students and teachers at other universities and arts centers throughout the country where I have taught poetry.

Through this book, I hope to give you the confidence that comes with increased writing and reading and believing in yourself. This book is intended to help you to overcome writer's block; it is intended to open you up to your own experience. It can be used in classrooms or to provide impetus for a group of writers or for the individual writer sitting alone in a kitchen or in an armchair or at a desk. It is a way of jumpstarting your creativity; it is a way to get permission to tell your secrets, to write your stories. It is a book about process, rather than craft.

In the pages that follow, I provide examples of my poetry and a list of suggested poetry books with the hope that in them you will find writing that speaks to you. You will find different poets to whom you respond; those poets, in turn, can help you open more doors inside yourself. You need to write every day and read every day. You need to read poetry from other centuries. You need to memorize poems. You need to fall in love with poetry, because I don't believe you can write poetry unless you do.

If there is one theme in this book, it is courage; the courage to plunge into these prompts. Use them at random; use them more than once. Hopefully, they will lead you to places held in memory, to the past, and the textures and smells and tastes of that past. Believe in yourself. Share your poems with other people, especially those who are also using this book.

Part One

Exploring the Cave:

How to Find the Stories You Have to Tell

Chapter 1

Finding the Poet Inside You

Poems hide in a place deep inside of you that I call the cave. The cave is guarded by a crow that whispers in your ear in the voice of every authority figure you've ever encountered. The crow tells you all the reasons why you can't write, shouldn't write. He tells you everything that's wrong with you: "You're stupid, lazy, awkward." Every negative comment ever made to you, every withering look is part of the crow's ammunition against you and your creative spirit.

In order to write, you have to get rid of the crow; you have to push him out of your way. Only then can you enter the cave where poems abide. In the cave are all your memories, good and bad, the past, every person you've ever known and loved or hated, everything you are afraid of in the world and in yourself. In the cave is your rage and your fury and your passion. You have to enter the cave to find all the stories you have to tell and all the poems you have to write. Obviously, this kind of writing takes courage, but it also will imbue your writing with a renewed energy and passion.

Throughout this book, I address the reader as you, because it helps me to imagine the person who is reading this book, a person who is looking for the magic words that will release him or her from the ropes of self-doubt and worry. I want you to feel my encouragement and enthusiasm for everything I know you can do, both in your writing and in your life. One of my students put this line on her screen saver:

MARIA BELIEVES IN YOU!!!

Every time she turned on her computer, the line would be there, reassuring her and knocking that crow off her shoulder.

I believe in the poems that hide inside you. To help you reach them, I have provided hundreds of writing prompts designed to help you to get to the cave, to find the stories you need to tell and the voice in which to tell them. *Writing Poetry to Save Your Life* will get you started. What you need is paper, a pen, and the willingness to take risks. Plan to write once a day for twenty minutes or if that seems too difficult, then plan to write three times a week. Block out twenty minutes, and allow for as much silence as possible. When my own children were young, I would get up in the middle of the night to write. For some people getting up very early in the morning works better, or writing just before going to bed. The main thing is make a schedule to write.

Once you've established a time for writing, then you have to be willing to tell the truth in your writing. Choose a prompt from the back of this book, and write whatever comes into your mind about the topic. Do not censor yourself. Do not try to revise as you go along. Let your mind go and let your pen move as it wishes. As you descend into the cave inside yourself, your subconscious mind will take over and you won't be in control. You have to be willing to let that happen. All revision should be saved for a later time.

For the many years that I've taught poetry workshops, I have used the following prompt as the first one that I give my students. Of all the prompts I've used, this one seems to be magic, to have the ability to open people up, to make them go to places in their poems that they've never gone to before.

Begin by writing about a person who is very important to you. The person has to be someone with whom you have a very long history – a mother, father, sister, brother, grandfather, grandmother, cousin, aunt, uncle. Imagine that person. Think about where you see the person when you think of him or her: in a kitchen stirring soup, wearing an apron, hands dusted with flour; in an office sitting at a desk with lamplight on his or her hair; in a barcalounger holding a drink. What cologne or perfume do you associate with the person? What other smells – flour, sugar, cinnamon, ink, dust, cigarette smoke? Pretend you are speaking directly to the person and tell that person something you would be afraid to say because you fear the person will be angry or will laugh or because you would be embarrassed. Start by describing the person. Example: *Ma, I remember you in your basement kitchen, you always cooking and baking, you in your homemade flour sack apron, you smelling of flour and sugar and cinnamon ...*

The purpose of these writing prompts is to help you to write the first draft of the poem. Use details and be as specific as possible. Sometimes, it helps to visualize the place or person about which or whom you are going to write. Where would the person be? What would the person be doing? What kind of clothes would the person wear? What expressions does the person have? What is the first thing you notice about this place or person or time? If you do this enough, it will become second nature to you.

Chapter 2

Learning to Let Go

Because of the way you have been trained in school, you are often dealing with the critic in your head, that voice that tells you what is wrong with everything you do, that voice that makes you doubt yourself.

To combat that voice, it's important to open up that notebook, look at the first clean page, and start to write. This process is hindered or destroyed by allowing yourself to worry about whether what you are writing is good or bad, polished or rough, acceptable to others or not. You have to believe that nothing matters at this stage of the process except the words that flow from your pen onto the page. Resist the temptation to revise as you go along. Instead, allow your subconscious mind to take over and write what happens when you do.

I've always believed that the wise old woman who lives in your belly, that one who operates on instinct, knows what you need to write, what stories you need to tell. When you let your mind control what you write, you lose the electricity and vitality of the initial impulse, the basic truth that the old woman knows, that truth that makes our writing powerful.

The Greeks believed that poets could hear the voices of the gods and had the ability to interpret their wishes. The Greeks understood that poets are born with one less layer of skin, and are open to what is true about being human, as well as courageous about stating those truths. Modern life is full of noise and busyness, which can distract you from discerning these truths. That's why it is an important part of the process to find stillness and quiet each day, so you can tap into that part of yourself where truth abides.

When confronting that blank page, you must allow yourself the freedom to loosen up. If you catch yourself changing lines, crossing out, going back to revise, you are not letting go. You cannot get to a deeper place inside yourself or in your writing, unless you're willing to trust your instincts. You cannot control this process with your mind.

I realized the importance of this when Diane di Prima and I were on a reading tour, and she suggested that I bring painting supplies. After we arrived at the hotel, she left me alone in my room to paint. I started to get very nervous when confronted by the blank drawing pad. My hands felt stiff and unnatural. I became increasingly upset that I couldn't draw a perfect rose even though I was staring at one in front of the window. I kept tearing off sheets and trying again, and finally I had a pile of muddied, blurred paintings.

Suddenly, I realized this is the very thing I cautioned my writing students against. I took a deep breath, and tried to let go, the way I had learned years ago with my writing. The painting did not have to be perfect; it did not have to be anyone else's idea of the perfect rose. I had to look at the world through my own eyes and paint it, the same way I did when writing a poem.

Once I realized that, I was able to paint, and my hand and wrist loosened; I was happy with my creation. I stopped worrying about whether it was good or bad. It didn't matter. What mattered was that I was painting and I was pleased because the colors and shapes were translations of what I saw in my mind.

The time alone in that room, I see now, was a gift. In writing, you must give yourself the same gift. Twenty minutes are enough to write a draft of a poem. Believe that, and your hand, too, will loosen up and you will be surprised and delighted by your own creation.

Chapter 3

Translating Our Lives

My mother spoke an Italian dialect mixed with her own version of English; she could not read English. In Italy, she went to school through the third grade; after that, she worked in the fields and cooked for her entire family. When she came to America she was already 24 years old and pregnant with my sister. It was the middle of the Depression, and they settled into the life of many new immigrants, my father working in a factory when he could get a job. He even worked with the WPA on street repair for a while. My mother worked hand-sewing the sleeves in coats. The factory would drop the coats off at the house in the morning and pick them up again the next morning, leaving behind other coats for her to sew. Even later, when we were in school, and she was able to work in Ferraro's coat factory, she worked with other Italian immigrants from her area of Italy and they chattered in their dialect while they sewed.

My mother had an intense desire to learn everything; she was quick and practical and efficient. She wanted to learn English and in order to do that she knew she had to go to night school. My father refused to allow it. Though she ranted and cried, he would not give in. "Women don't need to go to school," he insisted. Now, when I see how immigrants make a beeline for Passaic County Community College where they can get ESL classes and master Basic English, I think of how my mother would have given anything for such an opportunity. Although the opportunity was denied, she was well aware that language was power.

My mother had a padded rocker in which she would sit at night. We'd sit in her lap or the arm of the chair, and she would tell us Italian fairy tales or stories of her life in Italy before she came to America. I loved her rich laugh, her ability to spin a scary story or a hope-filled one, the music of that Italian dialect she spoke, and the English words she created when she didn't really know the English word for something.

But my mother was always ashamed of her illiteracy. There were so many things she could not do when confronted with Americans, who did not understand what she was saying, and she, my super-competent mother, became helpless as a child when faced with their rudeness and sense of superiority.

I remember once going to a department store with my mother when I was 14 or 15, and the sales clerk was rude to her, because she asked a question about some nylons. I saw that my mother was ready to slink away from that woman, to duck her head in shame, and I yelled at that clerk so everyone in the store turned to look at me. "Don't ever, ever talk to a customer that way again. I want to speak to your manager right now," I said. She got that manager for me and, in my perfect English, I told him what had happened. Because I was articulate and furious and suddenly more powerful than I had ever been in my shy, 15-year-old self, I realized the power of language to present my side of an argument and to make people listen. I realized, too, though my mother was very intelligent and quick-witted in Italian and in the realm of her domestic life, outside of the confines of that Italian neighborhood and house, she was dismissed as stupid and unimportant.

My mother could tell me her stories in Italian, but she could not tell them to America, and maybe that was part of the reason why I decided that I had to be a writer. I remember the Sunday I announced my ambition and my cousin, the accountant, said: *That's the most impractical ambition I've ever heard*. While part of me knew it was impractical for a working class girl, whose first language was Italian, another stubborn part of me knew I'd have to write in order to save the stories of my mother's and father's lives, to tell those stories to an America that would have to listen, whether it wanted to or not. Language gave me power, and I wasn't giving it up for anything.

Whenever my students whisper, I shout: *Speak up. Claim your voice. Seize your power.* I force them to raise their voices so everyone can hear. In a way, that's what happens when you write; you are seizing your power. Your words need to crackle. Sometimes, I get frightened that people will criticize me for what I'm writing. Then, I think of my mother in that department store who could not find the words to defend herself and I stiffen my spine and forge ahead.

In the same way Italian can be translated into English, we need to translate our inner lives, the place that we never talk to anyone about, into poems and stories and memoir in order to make the past come alive. Here is an example of such a poem about my grandmother, called "Donna Laura," which appears in my book, *What We Pass On: Collected Poems 1980-2009*.

Donna Laura

Donna Laura, they called my grandmother
when they saw her sitting in the doorway, sewing
delicate tablecloths and linens, hours of sewing
bent over the cloth, an occupation for a lady.

Donna Laura, with her big house falling
to ruins around her head,
Donna Laura, whose husband
left for Argentina when she was twenty-four,
left her with seven children and no money
and her life in that southern Italian village
where the old ladies watched her
from their windows. She could not have
taken a breath without everyone knowing

Donna Laura who each day sucked
on the bitter seed
of her husband's failure
to send money and to remember
her long auburn hair,

Donna Laura who relied on the kindness
of the priest's "housekeeper"
to provide food for her family.
Everyone in the village knew

my grandmother's fine needlework
could not support seven children,
but everyone pretended not to see.

When she was ninety, Donna Laura
still lived in that mountain house.
Was her heart a bitter raisin,
her anger so deep it could have cut
a road through the mountain?
I touch the tablecloth she made,

the delicate scrollwork,
try to reach back to Donna Laura,
feel her life shaping itself into laced patterns
and scalloped edges from all those years between
her young womanhood and old age.

Only this cloth remains,
old and perfect still, turning her bitterness into art
to teach her granddaughters and great granddaughters
to spin sorrow into gold.

Chapter 4

Trusting Yourself

A student called me the other night, worrying that her manuscript wasn't any good because she had just read a critic who denigrated personal poetry. Who wants to read about my family? Who cares? This critic said it was narcissistic to write about your own life. I reassured her. I asked her if she realized how quiet our workshop became when she read her poems, that stillness that only comes to a group when they are totally drawn into a poem. I realized after talking to her that I would have to include in this book a warning that there are lots of people talking the kind of drivel this critic is talking. I even asked her to read one of the critic's poems; it was a poem that was so imitative, so derivative of 19th century poetry that it was laughable. The language was stiff and unreal; the poem was just plain boring because he was unwilling to take a risk.

Allen Ginsberg told me that when he was a young man and was studying at Columbia, he was encouraged to write nature sonnets. He sent those poems to William Carlos Williams who asked him what he knew about pheasants and waterfowl. Williams encouraged him to write about Paterson, New Jersey, where he grew up and about his own life. Ginsberg, always sharp and a quick learner, went home and wrote *Howl* and *America* and *Kaddish* and changed American literature completely. I credit him with opening the door first for women poets and later for Black, Hispanic, Asian, and working class poets. Ginsberg read some of his sonnets to me, and believe me when I say that those poems would not have changed anything.

I want you to hear my voice in your head, when you begin to doubt what you're doing, when you're writing your life and your stories into your work: *believe in yourself.* Only poems that make you cry or laugh or make the hair on your arms stand up are worth writing. Anything else is just you trying to fit in, to be acceptable, to be what critics want you to believe a true poet is. I think of an article I read in the *New York Times* magazine several years ago. The premise of this article was that poetry has always been an elite art form; it has never been an art form that has attracted a large audience nor should it be. I say the opposite. I'm happy when I get letters and phone calls and emails about my work. I'm happy when someone comes up to me after a reading, and the person is crying and wants to tell me about his or her life. That means I've built a bridge between us and isn't that what literature is?

Don't let critics make you doubt yourself. You have stories to tell and you have the right to tell them. Don't believe them when they tell you that you don't. Don't let them stop you from writing because then they've won. They can believe that their esoteric poems are the only ones that should be written. I say I want to hear your story.

Tell me, again and again.

Part Two

Ways to Improve Your Writing

Chapter 5

Reading Poetry Aloud

When I was 16, my English teacher at East Side High School in Paterson, NJ, was Miss Durbin, the same English teacher who taught Allen Ginsberg. I was horribly shy and introverted, but Miss Durbin encouraged me to read poetry out loud to the class, indicating to me that she loved the way I read poetry. In reading those poems aloud, the poems of Tennyson and Blake and Keats, I learned that words had shape and texture; that reading poems aloud was a sensual experience, as sensual an experience as eating a sweet peach. In those moments when I was reading those poems, I forgot how shy I was, forgot myself and let the sound and music of those poems carry me away from everything gray and ordinary in my life.

I have never stopped loving the sound of poetry. I encourage you to buy poetry CDs to listen to in the car as you drive, so you can develop your ear for poetry. There is something exquisite about being in that enclosed, secret, safe world of the car while a poet's voice fills the space with the sound of poetry. I remember once driving an inner-city student home from poetry workshops, and when I put on a poetry tape for her, her face turned luminous and she cried. "I didn't know it could sound like that," she kept saying. "I didn't know."

Another way to help you develop your ear for poetry is to read your own poems out loud to yourself and to other people. Sometimes, it's possible to hear when a line doesn't work when you read a poem to an audience. Is there something flat in the line? Do you trip over a particular word? Is it possible another word would be better?

Writing poetry is not, after all, an intellectual exercise. It is rooted in the body and the body learns its lessons well. As a singer must listen to music, a poet needs to bathe in language, needs to let it enter through all the pores of the skin. You cannot write in a vacuum. You need to listen to poetry, to hear the beauty of the language.

But it isn't enough only to listen to poetry. It's important to read everything – novels, poems, cereal boxes, newspapers – and to listen to the way people talk, the cadence of the language you hear spoken by people in the diner or the symphony or the school. All of these things are part of the American voice and language, which you need to absorb through your eye and ear into your body. It will then always be there for you when you are writing, when you finally let go and let your pen move across that page, faster and faster as you go down inside yourself to the place where all poems hide.

The following poem, "Daddy, We Called You" from *What We Pass On*, speaks to language and cadence, shows the way we spoke – my brother, sister and I – inside and outside of our close-knit Italian-American family.

Daddy, We Called You

"Daddy," we called you. "Daddy,"
when we talked to each other in the street,
pulling on our American faces,
shaping our lives in Paterson slang.

Inside our house, we spoke
a Southern Italian dialect
mixed with English
and we called you Papa

but outside again, you became Daddy
and we spoke of you to our friends
as "my father"
imagining we were speaking
of that *Father Knows Best*

T.V. character
in his dark business suit,
carrying his briefcase into his house,
retreating to his paneled den,
his big living room and dining room,
his frilly-aproned wife
who greeted him at the door
with a kiss. Such space

and silence in that house.
We lived in one big room –
living room, dining room, kitchen, bedroom,
all in one, dominated by the gray oak dining table
around which we sat, talking and laughing,
listening to your stories,
your political arguments with your friends,
Papa, how you glowed in company light,
happy when the other immigrants
came to you for help with their taxes
or legal papers.

It was only outside that glowing circle
that I denied you, denied your long hours
as night watchman in Royal Machine Shop.
One night, riding home from a date,
my middle class, American boyfriend
kissed me at the light; I looked up
and met your eyes as you stood at the corner

near Royal Machine. It was nearly midnight.
January. Cold and windy. You were waiting
for the bus, the streetlight illuminating
your face. I pretended I did not see you,
let my boyfriend pull away, leaving you
on the empty corner waiting for the bus
to take you home. You never mentioned it,
never said that you knew

how often I lied about what you did for a living
or that I was ashamed to have my boyfriend see you,
find out about your second shift work, your broken English.

Today, remembering that moment,
still illuminated in my mind
by the streetlamp's gray light,
I think of my own son
and the distance between us,
greater than miles.

Papa,
silk worker,
janitor,
night watchman,
immigrant Italian,
I honor the years you spent in menial work
slipping down the ladder
as your body failed you

while your mind, so quick and sharp,
longed to escape,
honor the times you got out of bed
after sleeping only an hour,
to take me to school or pick me up;
the warm bakery rolls you bought for me
on the way home from the night shift.

The letters
you wrote
to the editors
of local newspapers.

Papa,
silk worker,
janitor,
night watchman,
immigrant Italian,

better than any *Father Knows Best* father,
bland as white rice,
with your wine press in the cellar,
with the newspapers you collected
out of garbage piles to turn into money
you banked for us,
with your mouse traps,
with your cracked and calloused hands,
with your yellowed teeth.
Papa,
dragging your dead leg
through the factories of Paterson,
I am outside the house now,
shouting your name.

Chapter 6

Keeping a Journal

When I was 8 years old, my sister received a book of fairy tales for her birthday. She was uninterested since she was practical and scientific, and didn't need fantasy in the same way that I did. I loved that book and while reading it I knew that reading was something I could never relinquish. I started walking to the Paterson Public Library's Riverside Branch on Madison Avenue. In grammar school, I read through the children's section and into the adult section under the encouraging eye of Christine, the librarian. I started with A and worked toward Z, picking up seven books, carting them home to read, and climbing the Madison Avenue hill once again the next week for seven more, the life inside those books more real to me than the life of 19th Street and the front stoop where, sitting on a wooden chair, my feet propped on the railing, I read the books. I read everything – the good, the bad, the mediocre, and I soon began to identify the writing that was unforgettable, the stories that made me cry or laugh.

As a child I rarely left Paterson and the Italian immigrant neighborhood where I grew up, so the world outside my very confined world was unfamiliar to me. My mother felt we were safe, as long as we stayed on our front stoop or in our backyard. She came to the United States from Italy when she was a young woman, and leaving this world of other Italian-speaking people was not something she ever wanted to do or see her children do. I think the trip to America in steerage, when she was five months pregnant, traumatized her so much that she tried to rebuild the confined world of her small village within our house. For me, books became a way of leaving behind the constraints of my mother's world, of following these characters to places I could only imagine, to experiences I longed to have, even though I was never a physically brave or athletic child.

I think that's why I loved the *Little House on the Prairie* books and the *Nancy Drew* mysteries. I read all those books many times because the lives pictured there were so different from my own and, while I was reading those books, I imagined I could be as brave as Nancy Drew, as courageous as the people in those covered wagons riding across the vast plains. How these books fueled my longing to escape from the world of 19th Street with its immigrant gardens and plaster statues of the Virgin Mary encased in homemade cement shrines. While I was reading, I could imagine in myself bravery I didn't have, a day when I, fearless and undaunted, would travel to distant places.

At 13, I went off to Eastside High School in Paterson, where I was fortunate to have Alfred Weiss and Frances Durbin as my English teachers. They taught me the classic writers, taught me to love them as they loved them. They also encouraged me to keep a journal. They suggested getting a stenographer's notebook and setting a time each day to write. Since then, I have always kept a journal and often my poems start in my journal. To keep the stream of language flowing, I write every day. Sometimes I use one of those beautiful books that are available now, leather-bound volumes with creamy pages; sometimes I use books that friends give me, small enough to carry in my purse. I always have more than one journal in which I write. Diane di Prima, the Beat poet who has become a close friend, showed me her journals in which she paints and does collage. Following her suggestion, I have begun to paint and do collage and to draw in my journals. The world of art is connected to that of writing.

When we go somewhere together, Diane and I bring paints and collage materials; we set aside time each day to write and to paint. Sometimes, we go to a museum together to allow contemporary American art or art of other countries and eras to be part of us. With her encouragement, I am trying to set aside time in my own life for moments like these – to allow the sights and sounds and smells of the world to enter the body – and I encourage my students to do the same.

Everything that happens, everything that you see and feel and touch, becomes a part of you and of your writing; the more you open yourself to the world, the more you will have to give back to that world through your writing. Get yourself a journal; it doesn't matter what kind it is. It should be a size and shape that feels comfortable for you. Write in it every day. Learn to look at the world as only you can, and translate that world into your journal.

Chapter 7

Go On a Retreat

Because contemporary life is so busy and full of things we feel we have to do, the time and space we need in order to write is often last on our list of priorities. It's important to make space for ourselves if we want to write. Often we don't feel we deserve this kind of space and time, and therefore, we are afraid to say no to that one more thing, one more obligation. I sometimes think that if I don't say "yes" to every request, people will stop asking me. Although my mind knows this fear is ridiculous, I find it extremely difficult to say "no," even to things I really don't want to do.

It is essential for all of us to believe that we are important, that we deserve time to ourselves. I recommend taking retreats. On these retreats, you don't necessarily need to go away. You can simply program your phone to say that you are on a retreat, "and won't be back until ..." Also, you can leave an out-of-office reply on your computer so that people will know you are unavailable. Once you do this, you will realize how much time you waste on the telephone and answering email, and acknowledge that it is time taken away from your interior life.

I use this time to write or just to stare into space. I call it rejuvenation therapy, and it has helped me enormously. I think you'll find it a blessing for you and for your writing. Somehow with all the things we take on in our lives, we soon begin to believe we must do everything, that if we aren't always rushing, our lives don't matter. These retreats are a way for you to take a fresh look at yourself. You'll be thrilled when you realize how much good they do you and your writing. Suddenly, the words that just wouldn't come, the ideas that seemed to turn to stone when you tried to reach for them, will begin to appear in your mind and will flow from your pen. We need this space, a space emptied of obligations, to allow our creative selves to emerge once again.

Jim Haba, poet, artist and former Poetry Director of the Geraldine R. Dodge Foundation, started a program in 1986, which was aimed at teachers. Called "Clearing the Spring, Tending the Fountain," the program is intended to open teachers up to the memory of why they first wanted to teach literature. This program, designed to make the participants feel a renewed comfort with language and poetry, has been enormously successful in generating teachers who are enthusiasts of poetry. These teachers become so excited by writing and reading poetry that they can't wait to share this love with their students.

Taking a retreat is a way of clearing your own spring of the debris of everyday life that keeps you from writing and thinking and creating. You will emerge from this space renewed and refreshed; once again you will be in touch with those instincts that brought you to love writing poetry in the first place.

Chapter 8

Read, Read, Read, and Read Some More

My granddaughter is growing up far away from me in Texas, but when I see her carrying her book with her wherever she goes, and how engrossed she gets in a story, I realize that people like my granddaughter and myself are drawn naturally to books. A reader is not something we decided to be. If I go on a trip, I know I can't leave home without packing several books to read when I get to where I'm going. Sometimes I've run out of books when I'm away, and I get really panicky until I can get to a bookstore to buy another one. Reading has become as necessary to me as breathing. I encourage you to develop the same need for books that I have; as this need will inform your writing as it has informed so much of mine.

That doesn't mean that you can't learn to be a reader, to find in books a basic comfort for the pain and sorrow in your life, to find in them a respite from the busy, mindless movement of modern life. I know firsthand that even someone who does not naturally gravitate toward books can learn to love them. As a young mother, I was anxious that my daughter did not seem interested in reading. I read to her, of course, since I believe that it's essential for parents to read to their children. There's something so incredibly wonderful about holding a child in your arms and reading. Such an early introduction to books is the first step to creating future readers. I tried to teach my daughter to read on her own as well, but she was a very active child who really didn't like to sit still long enough to read. I knew that I just had to find the right book to capture her attention. It took some trial and error to find the book that would really speak to her. For my daughter, the book was Judy Blume's *Are You There God? It's Me, Margaret*. She read it quickly and started asking for more. Now she, too, carries books with her wherever she goes.

Try to find the book that speaks to you. If you are not a person who has ever enjoyed reading, you can start with listening to *Selected Shorts* on Public Radio or to novels or non-fiction books on tape or CD. Soon, you will find yourself wanting to read the books for yourself. Quickly, you will see that your own writing is deepened and is strengthened by this reading.

There's one unbreakable law for every writer: *If you want to write, you have to read*. I'm not referring to reading one book a year, but rather to reading as many books as possible in any given year, and to reading at least a few pages every day. You need to read in order to help you explore your creative self. It doesn't matter so much what you read, just that you're driven to read, that reading should become as necessary to you as drinking water or eating.

I don't think you can write in a vacuum. You need to fill up your interior life with other writers' words and images, to go to museums, to drink in visual art and theater and music, because all of these things give your own work extra meaning. They are an unconscious way of teaching you how to write and how to open yourself to the world of words and language. All the characters and situations and feelings and thoughts in other people's books will become a part of your subconscious mind. They will always be a part of you, and you then can draw on the feelings and thoughts they elicit in you when you are writing. A weightlifter needs protein and carbs in large amounts to keep on lifting weights. The writer needs other people's words to keep going, to get the burn.

Read. Get the Burn. Be Inspired.

Chapter 9

Write It Down Immediately

Over so many years of writing, I've discovered that, if I don't write a poem down immediately when it comes to me, I end up losing it. I can never remember it later. Once many years ago when I was driving, a poem came to me and I started searching my car for something to write it down on. I finally found an envelope on the floor and I wrote the poem as I drove. Apparently, I was a danger to myself and everyone else on the road because the parish priest followed me to the bank where I was headed, and berated me for my erratic driving.

"I was writing a poem," I said.

"Maybe you should just do one thing at a time," he replied, giving me one of those looks that said he thought I was certifiable.

After that embarrassing experience, I keep a small notebook with a pen attached to it on a cord in the car. But, when I get an urge to write a poem, I pull over, no matter how tempted I am to write and drive. Also I keep the same kind of notebook near my bed and near the sofa where I sit to read or watch TV, and I carry one in my bag to use when I am sitting at a meeting that seems interminable. I suggest this method to you as well.

The problem with waiting to write until you have time or things are quieter is that you may find that you'll never have time to write. When my children were young and I didn't feel as though I had one minute to myself, I got up in the middle of the night to read and write. Of course, I was younger then and could go without sleep, but in those days, when my house was always full of children and noise and things to be done, my spirit needed the refreshment of that hour in the middle of the night more than it needed sleep.

Now that my children are grown and out of the house, I still have all sorts of professional and personal responsibilities pulling at me, as we all do. But again I say, if you do not make time for yourself and your writing, you won't write – ever. I think sometimes you're afraid that you will fail, so you don't try. Surely, you can find 20 minutes sometime in your day or night to write. No excuses. No get-out-of-writing-free card.

If you need extra help to get motivated, then join a group, even a group of two or three friends, and write together and read what you've written aloud to each other. I know a writer who gets a motel room, and stays there a weekend each month to write. You can get together with one other person whose taste and sensibility you trust, and write poems together or read each other's work. My students often tell me that they love the intensive weekends I lead at Binghamton, because it forces them to write nine or ten poems over the course of the weekend. It may take some trial and error but, if you keep trying different approaches, you will find the one that is most effective for you.

I don't allow myself or anyone else to say, "I don't have time." If you want to write, if you want to explore your own creativity, you have to make the time. *Excuses are for cowards who are afraid to try*, I say to myself when I'm looking for a reason to explain why I haven't written. Don't use that excuse for yourself.

Part Three

How to Make Your Writing Come Alive

Chapter 10

Poetic Voice

What is poetic voice? How do you find it in other people's poems? How do you find it in yourself? Thinking about this topic, I realize that it is more complicated than it seems. We can look at the poems of someone like Marie Howe or Gerald Stern or Ruth Stone, and you can ask yourself: What is it that is characteristic of their poems? What is the sound of their poems? Take for example, Gerald Stern's "The Dancing." What are the characteristics of the voice in this poem? What picture of the poet and speaker emerges in the poem? Is the voice in the poem philosophical, down-to-earth or lyrical? All of the above?

Look at Ruth Stone's poem, "Names." What are the characteristics of this poem? What is the effect of the seemingly unconnected or random thoughts in the poem? What other characteristics are a part of the voice of the poem? Let's look at Marie Howe's poem, "The Boy," as an example. What is the primary feeling that you get about the speaker in this poem? How does the subject enhance the voice? How does the length of the line contribute to poetic voice?

If the voice in a poem is strong and unique, then you should be able to find words to describe it and it should be recognizable, even if the person's general style or subject matter changes. See if you can describe the voice in this poem, "Public School No. 18, Paterson, New Jersey," from *What We Pass On*.

Public School No. 18, Paterson, New Jersey

Miss Wilson's eyes, opaque
as blue glass, fix on me:

"We must speak English.
We're in America now."
I want to say, "I am American,"
but the evidence is stacked against me.

My mother scrubs my scalp raw, wraps
my shining hair in white rags
to make it curl. Miss Wilson
drags me to the window, checks my hair
for lice. My face wants to hide.

At home, my words smooth in my mouth,
I chatter and am proud. In school,
I am silent, grope for the right English
words, fear the Italian word
will sprout from my mouth like a rose,

fear the progression of teachers
in their sprigged dresses,
their Anglo-Saxon faces.

Without words, they tell me
to be ashamed.
I am.
I deny that booted country
even from myself,
want to be still
and untouchable
as these women
who teach me to hate myself.

Years later, in a white
Kansas City house,
the Psychology professor tells me
I remind him of the Mafia leader
on the cover of *Time* magazine.

My anger spits
venomous from my mouth:

I am proud of my mother,
dressed all in black,
proud of my father
with his broken tongue,
proud of the laughter
and noise of our house.

Remember me, Ladies,
the silent one?
I have found my voice
and my rage will blow
your house down.

In trying to develop your own voice, you have to pay attention to
the voice that you hear in your own head. When William Carlos
Williams advocated using the American idiom and rooting poems
in a given place, I think that's what he meant. While you should
read a great deal of poetry and listen to poetry, in the end, you have
to get in tune with your own life, and what's important to you and
how the language sounds to you.

Chapter 11

Specificity

In the mid-seventies when I had already been writing and publishing poetry for many years, I sent some poems to Ruth Lisa Schechter, the editor of the *Croton Review*. She wrote back to me, saying she'd like to talk to me about my poetry and asking me to visit her. In the years that I had been publishing, no editor had ever asked me to visit so I was thrilled. I immediately called her and made an appointment to meet with her.

At her house in Croton-on-Hudson, she sat with me for more than three hours, and explained that my poetry was strong, but it could be much stronger. It lacked, she told me, specificity. Line by line, she went over a poem I had written about my father, pointing out each place where I had been less than specific and asking me questions about my father. She also advised me to read Allen Ginsberg's "Kaddish." She said I could learn a great deal about specificity if I'd read that poem.

I have always been grateful to Ruth for spending that time with me, for providing me with the push I needed to get me to take bigger risks in my work. It's the same kind of help I've tried to provide to writers and to students. Sometimes we are insulted when people try to tell us the truth about our work; after all, our poems are like our children. Do we want anyone to say *that is one ugly baby*? No, of course not, and driving home from Croton-on-Hudson, I was no more ready to hear what Ruth was telling me about my work than anyone else would have been. But I immediately bought Ginsberg's book and read it all the way through, and then, I looked at my own poem and realized it was too general. My poem could have been about anyone's father. I went back and re-wrote that poem for months until I was satisfied that this was a poem about my father and that he could not be mistaken for anyone else. The result was the following poem, called "Betrayals," which appeared in *What We Pass On.*

Betrayals

At thirteen, I screamed,
"You're disgusting,"
drinking your coffee from a saucer.
Your startled eyes darkened with shame.

You, one dead leg dragging,
counting your night-shift hours,
you, smiling past yellowed, gaping teeth,
you, mixing the eggnog for me yourself
in a fat dime store cup,

how I betrayed you,
over and over, ashamed of your broken tongue,
how I laughed, savage and innocent,
at your mutilations.

Today, my son shouts,
"Don't tell anyone you're my mother,"
hunching down in the car
so the other boys won't see us together.

Daddy, are you laughing?
Oh, how things turn full circle,
my own words coming back
to slap my face.

I was sixteen when you called one night from your work.
I called you "dear,"
loving you in that moment
past all the barriers of the heart.
You called again every night for a week.

I never said it again.
I wish I could say it now.

Dear, my Dear,
with your twisted tongue,
I did not understand you
dragging your burden of love.

Try to picture the person you are writing about – try to see, hear, touch, smell that person. Picture the place you associate with the person. Pretend you're a camera, a video camera that has a sense of smell and touch. Quick! What do you see? What do you smell? What is the person doing?

Go to "Kaddish," the poem to which Ruth sent me. If any poem can teach us about the willingness to take risks and about specificity, this poem can do it. Next, go to Robert Hayden's "Those Winter Sundays," a short poem, but one in which Hayden allows us to know his father. Sections of "Kaddish" are available on the internet, and Hayden's poems are available there, as well.

A poem has to be rooted to the earth. It is the details, the specificity of the poem that roots it to the ground and pulls the reader in. I think what we all want as poets is to have people remember our work, to have that work become a part of someone else. I carry the poems I love with me wherever I go. I want people to remember my work, and write to me about it years after they've first read it or heard me read it. I want that experience for you, as well. I know I'm listening to or reading a failed poem, when my mind drifts away while I'm reading or listening. The details are the magic ingredient in poems. You cannot make a poem without them.

Chapter 12

Don't Worry – Form Doesn't Matter

Often students come into a class believing that poems have to rhyme and that only poems that rhyme are real poems. I want you to think of poetry as a very elastic form. The line between poetry and prose has eroded so that a poem can be one word on a line or ten-word lines or twenty-word lines or it can be blocked out so it looks like a square paragraph. Try not to concentrate on form, but rather on content. Let the poem be what it wants to be. Get that first draft down on paper. This advice also applies to personal essays, memoir, and even to English compositions. The first and most important thing is to get the content on paper.

Sometimes in a composition class, when I have been confronted by someone who simply cannot get the first word written on paper, I give the following advice: *Say your essay into a tape recorder and then write it down.*

You might be more articulate in speaking about your experiences than you are in writing them. At some point in your life, you lost confidence in yourself and the written word. I want to restore that confidence, the confidence that you can write, to get you past the block that keeps you staring at that blank page for 20 minutes before you can put down the first word. I want you to get past the point in which you are so frozen with fear that your pen remains stiff in your hands, and you are unable to write even one sentence without changing and crossing out your words.

To get past this point, you need to try the 20-minute focus. You need to spend 20 minutes putting pen to paper, letting anything you are thinking just flow onto the page. If you'll let go, if you stop trying to control the secret writer inside you, you will be able to say what you need to say in 20 minutes. If you find yourself correcting and crossing out, stop immediately and just let the words flow from your pen without judgment.

Chapter 13

Simplicity

In 1980, I had to pick up William Stafford at the airport to drive him to a reading that he was doing for me at the Poetry Center. Quickly, I realized that he was very upset because a critic had called his writing "simple." During his reading he gave a brilliant talk on simplicity and the difficulty of achieving it in writing. I've always felt that the simpler something appears, the harder it is to do.

Recently a student sent me a poem she had written in response to a prompt. The poem had some good, clear lines in it, but it was wrapped in complicated imagery and fifty-dollar words. The poem also made very tentative dips toward real emotion, and then ran away from it through its use of an elaborate extended metaphor that seemed stiff and forced. When I pointed this fact out to her, she was reluctant to get rid of most of the esoteric language, and the screen she had built with deliberately obscure language. I finally went through the poem cutting it down to the bone, paring away all the obscure language and most of the complicated metaphor. This student, having been schooled in a Ph.D. literature program, felt that it wasn't a poem if it didn't have all this extra clothing on it.

I thought back to William Stafford standing on the stage in the Passaic County Community College Theater, and talking about the simplicity of his poems. I think of my own poems, the ones I wrote thirty years ago which suffered from the deliberately obscure Greek god reference syndrome, and the ones I write today that are as direct and honest and plain as I can make them. I think of William Stafford's poem, "Our Kind."

In such a concise poem, he is able to explore complex feelings without making the reader feel that he or she is too stupid to understand the poem.

I sometimes think that some people writing today – whole schools of people, in fact – are writing for five people at an Ivy League school. These are the ones who bemoan the fact that their books don't sell. They are also the same ones who denigrate Garrison Keillor's *Writer's Almanac*, that NPR program in which he reads one poem a day. They denigrate it because the poems Keillor reads are comprehensible and appeal to a large audience.

Personally, I am grateful to Garrison Keillor for that program, for making poetry available to a large number of people and for helping to overcome the stereotype of poetry as incomprehensible, that stereotype that has haunted poetry for years. I'm also grateful on a personal level, because he has read my poems many times on his program, which back in 2005, resulted in *Italian Women in Black Dresses* going into its third printing less than a year after it was published. It also led to emails and phone calls from people across the country. Is that what I want? You bet I do. Even Shakespeare wrote for people in the pit, the ones who bought tickets to stand through the performance, as well as for the people who could afford expensive seats.

What Stafford was trying to say about his work is important to remember. Anyone can drape an idea or a feeling in yards of gauze and fluff; it's much harder to pare away the excess to reach the heart of the poem. Often a beginning poet marks himself or herself as a beginner by choosing the more esoteric word rather than the simpler word to express an idea. This method only makes the poem stiff and unnatural sounding. The following poem, "My Daughter at Fourteen: Christmas Dance," from *What We Pass On* is an example of a poem that uses simple language to convey an experience.

My Daughter at Fourteen: Christmas Dance

Panic in your face, you write questions
to ask him. When he arrives,

you are serene, your fear
unbetrayed. How unlike me you are.

After the dance,
I see your happiness; he holds
your hand. Though you barely speak,
your body pulses messages I can read

all too well. He kisses you goodnight,
his body moving toward yours, and yours
responding. I am frightened, guard my
tongue for fear my mother will pop out

of my mouth. "He is not shy," I say. You giggle,
a little girl again, but you tell me he
kissed you on the dance floor. "Once?"
I ask. "No, a lot."

We ride through rain-shining 1 a.m.
streets. I bite back words which long
to be said, knowing I must not shatter your
moment, fragile as a spun-glass bird,

you, the moment, poised on the edge of
flight, and I, on the ground, afraid.

You need to ask yourself when you're revising whether this word is one you would use when you are speaking or is it one you are using because you think it's poetic. Read it out loud to yourself. Record yourself. How does it sound to you? Do you sound like the person you really are or like the person you think you should be?

Sometimes I read poems in anthologies and journals, and I feel depressed because the poems sound like bad imitations of 19th Century English poetry. Obviously, the person writing them is afraid to use his or her own ears to listen to the sounds of American English or to let go enough to allow his or her own voice to come through. Don't lean on the crutch of archaic language. As an American writing in the 21st century, please don't betray yourself by writing as though you lived in 19th Century England.

Chapter 14

Poetry by Example

One poem written by a contemporary poet, Joe E. Weil, "Ode to Elizabeth," embodies all the suggestions I have given you in this book.

Ode to Elizabeth

"Grimy Elizabeth," *Time* magazine intones.
This city escaped the race riots
Never quite sank
And, consequently, never rose.

It's not a town for poets.
You live here, you work the factory or a trade.
Down the burg, in Peterstown,
Italian bricklayers sit
on stoops, boxes, chairs,
playing poker
into one a.m.

Drive up Elizabeth Avenue
and you'll hear the salsa music blast from every window.
Even the potted geraniums dance.
In La Palmita, old Cuban guys sip coffee
from little plastic cups.
They talk politics, prizefights, Castro,
soccer, soccer, soccer.

Our Mayor looks like a lesser Mayor Daley:
smokes cigars, wears loud plaid suits,
the penultimate used car salesman.
He's been in since '64, a Mick with a machine.
He's been re-elected because he's a consistent evil
and, here in Elizabeth, we appreciate consistency.

Half the law of life is hanging out, hanging on
to frame houses, pensions.
Every Sunday, ethnic radio: Irish hour, Polish hour,
Lithuanian hour. My father sits in the kitchen
listening to Kevin Barry.
He wishes he could still sing.
Two years ago, they cut his voice box out:
cigarettes, factory, thirty years' worth of
double shifts. My father's as grimy as Elizabeth,
as sentimental, crude.
He boxed in the Navy, bantamweight.
As a kid I'd beg him to pop a muscle
and show off his tattoo.

We are not the salt of the earth.
I've got no John Steinbeck illusions.
I know the people I love have bad taste
in furniture. They are likely to buy
crushed-velvet portraits of Elvis Presley
and hang them next to the Pope.
They fill their lives with consumer goods,
leave the plastic covering on sofas
and watch *Let's Make a Deal*.

They are always dreaming the lottery number
that almost wins.
They are staunch Democrats who voted for Reagan.
They are working class, laid off when
Singer's closed, stuck between chemical dumps and oil
refineries in a city where Alexander Hamilton
once went to school.

In the graveyard by the courthouse,
lie Caldwells, Ogdens, Boudinots.
Milton is quoted on their graves.
Winos sleep there on summer afternoons
under hundred-year-old elms.
They sleep on the slabs of our Founding Fathers
and snore for History.

The Irish of Kerry Head have vanished,
but up in Elmora, you still can see
the Jewish families walking home from synagogue.
They are devout, they are well dressed,
They read the Talmud.

Twelve years ago, I used to go to the Elmora Theater
with twenty other kids.
It was a run-down movie house that never
got the features till they'd been out a year.
Because the Elmora was poor, it showed
foreign films; art films we didn't know were art:
Fellini, Wertmuller, Bergman.
It cost a dollar to get in.

We'd sit there, factory workers' kids, half hoods,
watching *Amarcord*.
When the uncle climbed the tree
in Amarcord and screamed, "I want a woman!"
we all agreed.
For weeks, Anthony Bravo went around school
screaming, "I want a woman!" every chance he got.
I copped my first feel there,
saw *Hester Street, The Seduction of Mimi*.
Once they had a double feature:
Bruce Lee's *Fists of Fury* with Ingmar Bergman's
The Seventh Seal.

I remember, two hundred kids exploding
when Jack Nicholson choked the nurse

in *Cuckoo's Nest*.
Sal Rotolo stood up, tears streaming down his face,
and when they took Jack's soul away,
we all sat there silent.
It lingered with us all the way home,
empty-eyed and sad.

Here in Elizabeth, the tasteless city,
where *Amarcord* was allowed to be just another flick,
where no one looked for symbols,
or sat politely through the credits.
If Art moved us at all, it was with real amazement;
We had no frame of reference.

And so I still live here,
because I need a place where poets are not expected.
I would go nuts in a town where everyone read Pound,
where old ladies never swept their stoops
or poured hot water on the ants.

I am happiest in a motley scene,
stuck between Exxon and the Arthur Kill ...
I don't think Manhattan needs another poet.
I don't think Maine could use me.
I'm short, I'm ugly, I prefer Mrs. Paul's Fish Sticks
to blackened redfish.
I don't like to travel because I've noticed
no matter where you go, you take yourself with you,
and that's the only thing I care to leave behind.

So I stay here.
At night, I can still hear mothers yelling,
"Michael, supper! Get your ass in gear!"
Where nothing is sacred, everything is sacred;
Where no one writes, the air seems strangely
charged with metaphor.

In short, I like a grimy city.
I suspect Culture because it has been given over
to grants, credentials, and people with cute haircuts.
I suspect Poetry because it talks to itself
too much, tells an inside joke.
It has forgotten how to pray.
It has forgotten how to praise.

Tonight, I write no poem. I write to praise.
I praise the motley city of my birth.
I write to be a citizen of Elizabeth, New Jersey.
Like a goddamned ancient Greek, I stand for this smallest
bit of ground, my turf, this squalid city.
Here, in the armpit of the beast.

Tonight, the ghosts of Ogdens, Caldwells, Boudinots
walk among the winos.
They exist in the salsa music blaring on Elizabeth Avenue.
They rise up and kiss the gargoyles of Cherry Street.
They are like King David dancing naked
unashamed before the covenant.

Tonight, even the stones can praise.
The Irish dead of Kerry Head are singing in their sleep.
And I swear, the next time someone makes a face,
gives me that bite the lemon look, as if to say,
"My Gawd ... how can you be a poet and live
in that stinking town?"
My answer will be swift:
I'll kick him in the balls.

Reprinted with permission of the author from Identity Lessons, edited by Maria Mazziotti Gillan and Jennifer Gillan, Penguin Putnam Inc., New York, 1999.

If you read this poem, even once, there are phrases and lines that will stay with you because Weil has so clearly and completely described his world, the world he grew up in, that he forces you to remember your own early worlds, as well. His combination of the language of ordinary speech, and of the street with the lyrical language reminiscent of Dylan Thomas, really works in this poem, because the poem is so honest, so unpretentious. He describes his father: *My father sits in the kitchen/ listening to Kevin Barry. / He wishes he could still sing./ Two years ago, they cut his voice box out.*

He goes on to describe his people, the people of Elizabeth, New Jersey. *I know the people I love have bad taste/ in furniture. They are likely to buy/ crushed-velvet portraits of Elvis Presley/ and hang them next to the Pope./ They fill their lives with consumer goods,/ leave the plastic covering on sofas/ and watch Let's Make a Deal./ They are always dreaming the lottery number/ that almost wins.* The specificity of these descriptions makes us remember a certain place or group of people.

How could we forget the old ladies pouring hot water on the ants or the poet who prefers Mrs. Paul's fish sticks to blackened redfish? Or forget when he tells us: *I don't like to travel because I've noticed/ no matter where you go, you take yourself with you,/ and that's the only thing I care to leave behind.*

Read this poem several times. Look at your own work. When you use details, are they ones that are totally your own, as Joe Weil's details are his?

Part Four

Learning Courage

Chapter 15

What Will People Say?

The whole time I was growing up my mother always used the question, *what will people say if they find out or if they see you?* as a way of keeping us all in line. In Italian culture there is a concept called, *mala* or *brutta figura*, and my mother was a great believer in avoiding *mala figura* at all costs. Quite simply translated *mala figura* means bringing shame down on your family, making them look bad and embarrassing them and yourself.

I should not have been surprised, therefore, when my first book was published, and my mother was horrified: "Why can't you write poems like the kind of poems that are on the backs of funeral cards? Why can't you write beautiful poems about nature like the poems I memorized in Italy? Why can't you make up a life for us that is a life of leisure and wealth? Don't write about me. Don't tell my secrets."

Every time one of my students asks: "How can I write about that? My mother will be angry. My father will be upset. My sister will be annoyed." This makes me think of my mother standing on the basement stairs, anger evident in her face, when she told me not to write about her anymore. And I tell myself, what I always tell my students: *This story is your story; it is the world seen through your eyes.*

The people you describe are people who are part of your world, and if you deny your obligation to write about that world, you're denying yourself and all the writers who went before you, the writers who gave you permission to tell your story. If you start censoring yourself, telling the story the way others wish it could have been, you destroy the writing. It becomes a lie and it loses its power to move others to laughter or tears.

After my first book came out, my sister Laura, who was the nurse in my brother's office, placed copies of the book in the waiting room. Since they kept getting stolen, she finally wrote in black magic marker on the cover: OFFICE COPY: DO NOT REMOVE.

That stopped the books from disappearing. One day my mother, who was certain that no one else could clean my brother's office the way she could, got busy with her vacuum and her mop at a time when she thought only my sister would be there. She tied a rag around her head and put on her biggest apron and proceeded to move in her usual whirlwind fashion through the office. Suddenly, she looked up and saw a patient sitting in the waiting room. The woman asked my mother if the author of the book was related to the doctor. My mother whispered: "I think it's his sister," and scuttled out of that office and never went back to clean for him again.

It wasn't until one of my books was published in Italian and English that my mother seemed to understand and forgive me for writing about her. I think about how Thomas Wolfe's mother refused to talk to him again after he published *Look Homeward, Angel*, a book I loved and read over and over when I was a young woman. I'm glad he didn't decide to not publish that book. I think he knew how important it would be to another generation of young people, capturing as he did that longing and loneliness we all felt as we were growing up.

Once I became courageous enough to write about my life, influenced as I was by Anne Sexton and Sylvia Plath and Adrienne Rich, I couldn't go back to poems that imitated Keats and Shelley and that were not from the center of my own life. This is not to say that in fiction you can't create characters that are parts of many people you've known or that you can't write a narrative poem in the same way. It is important, however, to tell the truth about what you know concerning what it means to be human. And in a poem, if you are using the first person and writing as though the speaker in the poem is yourself, you can't get away with lying or pretending that you are something other than what you actually are. Even in fiction, if you lie about what you know to be true about human nature, your reader will sense it and will refuse to be drawn into the character's life.

The following poem, "What I Can't Face About Someone I Love" from *What We Pass On*, is about my relationship with my son. Even in the title, I try to speak to how important it is to tell the truth in our writing, no matter how painful that may be.

What I Can't Face About Someone I Love

That my son loves me but would prefer
not to see me too much. Every Sunday night,

when I call him in North Carolina where
he lives with his wife and two children,

I can hear the heaviness in his voice,
his "Hello" tempered with impatience,

our conversation stiff and stilted, though
I always think I can talk to a stone.

Strangers in buses and trains tell me their life
histories, acquaintances tell me about their affairs

and shattered marriages, show me the secret
undersides of their lives. My graduate students vie

for my attention. They want to sit next to me
and carry my bags and fetch my lunch,

but my son can't wait to get off the phone
with me. I ask him how the kids are

or specific questions about school, ask about

his wife, his job. He answers with one or two
words; "They're fine," or "Okay," or "The same."

My son is a lawyer; he was always brilliant
with language, at least written language,

and he can read a three-hundred page book
in an hour and remember every detail,

but with me he turns mute as a stump.
If I ask for help with some legal problem,

he will give it, but I do not hear in his voice
the lilt I hear in my daughter's voice

when I call her. Instead I hear reluctance,
as though his attention were focused

on some truly fascinating person
and he can't wait to get off the phone.

I tell stories that I hope will amuse him,

but finally, after struggling and finding no response,
I can't wait to hang up.

I say, "Well, John, have a good week.
Give everyone a hug for me." I know my son

has divorced me, somewhere deep inside
himself in a place he doesn't look at.

I am too much for him, too loud, too dramatic,
too frantic, too emotional. I laugh too much.

I wear him out in a minute and a half. If he never
saw me again he wouldn't miss me and this is what

I can't face about someone I love.

Here, is another poem, called "What a Liar I Am," also from *What We Pass On*, that exposes the lies I routinely told myself and my husband during his lengthy illness with Early Onset Parkinson's Disease.

What a Liar I Am

I have been lying for a long time now,

the sicker you get the more I lie
to myself most of all. I cannot say
how angry I am that this illness
is another person in our house, so lies
are the only way to get through each day.

How hard it is to admit that I am often
impatient and raging and that anger
is a pit I can never swallow, that love,
even mine for you who have been with me
forty years, cannot dissolve the hank
of loneliness that has become lodged

in my throat, the irritating squeaking
of your electric wheelchair, the way
I want to run from the putrid smell
of medicines rising from your skin,
the way I lie and lie so you won't know

how heavy this illness feels. How long
it has been going on, sixteen years now.
Your feet dragging along the carpet
on days you can still walk,
are like a fingernail on a blackboard.
"This is all too much for you," you say,
and I reassure you, "No, not for you,

nothing is too much for you."
"I am a burden you say,"
and "No, no" I say. "Not a burden."
The face I see in my mirror is not one
I want to see. Oh love, I could not
have imagined it would come to this,

when I can only live by lying to myself
and you, you with your begging eyes,
your reedy voice a clanging bell that calls me,
you whom I love but cannot carry.

I remember Marie Howe speaking at a conference once, and she told a story about her brother who said to her: "But it didn't happen that way." She responded: "It's my poem and it's the way I remember it." I want to say that my poems are drawn from my personal cache of memories, and I have to be as true to those memories as I can, even if maybe I've forgotten something or got it wrong. It has to feel true to me as I'm writing it, and hopefully, then, people will say, as my cousin Carmela did: "You got it perfectly. You really caught it. That's what it was like. Exactly."

A word of caution is necessary here, however. While I am encouraging you to be brave in your writing, there is a difference between writing and publishing. When you're ready to publish a book in which you've written about a living person, be sure to consider that person's likely reaction. Will he or she be offended or embarrassed? Use common sense. If the voice in your head says, *This could cause you trouble,* you may want to think about leaving that part out. I suggest that you set aside the poem for a while and then take a fresh look before making a decision.

Chapter 16

Writing What You Know

My early experiences with stories and poems came in the form of the *Dick and Jane* books which I loved, but which also filled me with longing for a life totally different from my own. I remember clearly, the books painted in primary colors, the cute Dick, and cute Jane and cute Spot with their big white colonial house, where even the doghouse was perfect. Their lives bore no resemblance to my own, but they were people I wanted to be. They were great motivators for a working class child to want to join the blessed ranks of the upper middle class. I might just as well have been longing to go to the moon. Still, reading those books in first grade was the part of school I loved best.

The teachers I remember with gratitude, however, were the ones who by third grade read poems and stories aloud to us. I don't think I would have written anything without them, because they made me realize how language and music are inextricably connected. I loved listening to them read those poems by Shelley and Wordsworth, James Greenleaf Whittier and Robert Frost, Longfellow and Tennyson, though the world of those poems was not my world either. I loved listening to them anyway, because my parents couldn't read to me in English and I loved the sound of English read aloud by these women who I thought were upper class. To this day, I love to have others read to me, and sometimes I ask my granddaughter to read to me since she has always read aloud beautifully, even when she was only 7 or 8 years old. Listening to those poems read aloud by my teachers in the gray winter classrooms of Public School No. 18 with its scratched chalkboards and dusty windowsills, I formed the desire in me to write and to create something as beautiful as these writers had. Very early, when I was 7 or 8, I started trying to write poems in imitation of the ones I was reading or of the ones printed in children's textbooks.

My first poem was published when I was 13 years old. It was a poem about a dog wagging its tail. It rhymed and was dreadful, but it was published in St. Anthony's Messenger. In our own little Italy, I became mildly famous for having a poem published in a real magazine. My mother was the original Mrs. Clean, and she thought animals were dirty and germ-laden so I didn't even have a dog. I didn't know anything at all about dogs. I didn't even know any dogs personally, so I broke the cardinal rule of writing by writing about something I knew nothing about. When I read the poem in the magazine, even I knew just how bad it was. I was determined that I would always write what I knew.

The following poem published in the North American Review is a good example of something that was all too familiar in my life in the 70s – the color orange!

What Was I Thinking?

In 1972, I loved orange, a color I thought suited me
as blue did my blonde sister-in-law. So when I replaced
the dirty pinky-gray carpet that came with our house,
I bought a deep-orange shag, the living room and dining
room both large rooms, covered in acres of bright orange

carpet. To add to the effect, I painted the walls harvest moon,
a lighter shade than the carpet but still orange
after all, and last, I bought a deep orange chair
and an orange cheese platter with a sunflower painted
in the middle where I plopped a slab of orange cheddar

and surrounded it with crackers and served it to the other
couples who visited us on Saturday evenings – Judy and Al,
Mary Ellen and Vic, Laura and Fred, Bob and Bette.
For the final touch, I added an orange fondue pot
with a flame cup under it. Inside, melted orange cheddar

cheese I served with French bread. Perfect! In my bright
orange universe, I thought I had arrived, moved away
from the drab tenement where I grew up, the colorless
world of my mother's house. I dressed in a long skirt
and silk blouse, or bell-bottom lounging pants

and blouses with balloon sleeves secured by tight cuffs
at the wrist. Dennis wore a shirt with flowers on it,
a tapered shirt that showed off his wide shoulders
and narrow waist. The children peeked at us from
the curve in the stairs. We had gin and tonic
and scotch and soda and we'd talk and laugh.
I thought I was sophisticated and rising
toward the upper class. The brightness of those rooms
felt as if I had taken the sun and brought it inside, which,
because of the big oaks that surrounded our house,
was always dark. Imagine us there together, both of us,
32 years old, our children finally asleep in their beds,
surrounded by our friends,
we had so much of our lives ahead of us, the future
we are certain is as bright and full of possibilities
as the room. Nothing can stop us. We cannot imagine
a time when we will look back
at ourselves and laugh at how much
we had yet to learn, how little we knew.

Chapter 17

The Dangers of Concentrating on Publication

As I entered high school, I began to read a lot of the imagist poets and the translations in *One Hundred Poems from the Japanese* by Kenneth Rexroth. Those poems influenced me tremendously. In fact, I believe writing haiku after haiku taught me how to use imagery in my poems. I also read and studied the imagist poets such as Amy Lowell and Carl Sandburg. I learned from all this reading how to use imagery in a natural way, so that it was as though I had absorbed the images through all the pores of my skin. Years later, as the style of my poems changed, I dropped almost all of the imagery; I tried to use more of the language of ordinary speech in my poems. But at 16, I was truly bitten by the writing bug when two pages of my imagistic poems were published in a glossy magazine. That publication encouraged me and helped me to believe in myself. It also solidified my desire to be a writer.

The danger, I think, of connecting writing with publication is that you can end up focusing on writing in a way that will be acceptable and publishable. If you concentrate on publication possibilities when you're writing, I think you lose your focus on the writing itself. Instead of the process of writing – the desire to shape our experience into language that can form a bridge between your life and that of others – you concentrate on what is bland and acceptable. You become afraid to take any risks in your work.

When you're writing, you need to concentrate on the poem or story you are writing; you need to find the voice inside yourself that fits the poem or story and that is honest and true to the story. Publication is important. We all like to be published and to win prizes and awards. It validates us and our work, but in the end, it is the writing that matters. If it's any good, it will last long after no one remembers the names of any prize, no matter how prestigious.

I could paper ten rooms with rejections slips and contest letters informing me I didn't win, but I don't care about it as much as I did 20 years ago. I have to believe in what I'm doing with my work and where that work needs to go, even if no one else agrees. I know that I'm on a journey and that I have to follow wherever my instinct about writing leads me. I can't worry who likes what I'm doing and who doesn't. I hope that the readers of this book will learn much more quickly what it has taken me so many years to learn. Your instincts know more about what you need to write than anyone who exists outside of your skin.

Chapter 18

The Tough Subjects

What I am asking you to do in this book is to shed your inhibitions, to shut out the voice of the crow, who keeps telling you that you can't write about that subject, whatever it is, because it's too frightening or too sad or too shameful. I felt it was important for me to show you an example of a poem that for me was one of the most difficult I've ever written. For anyone who has been long married or partnered, there are a lot of taboo subjects. These are taboos we place on ourselves, because we want to think of ourselves as kind and supportive and loving, no matter how many times we know we fall short of that ideal. We want to believe the best of ourselves, but deep down we also know that we often can't meet our eyes in the mirror, the person that mirror reveals us to be.

When I wrote this poem, published in *What We Pass On*, I was thinking about shame. I had no idea where it was going; it had its own direction and my pen simply followed. While it started as a childhood memory of my embarrassment in front of my grown-up male cousin, before I knew it, I was heading toward an entirely different source of shame.

Shame

Today I was thinking about shame and how much
it is a part of everything we do, the way
I was ashamed at 10 to say to my cousin
that my mother asked me to buy toilet paper,

as though my grown-up male cousin didn't use
toilet paper and wasn't stuck with all those messy bodily
functions we have to plan our lives around, the way public
bathrooms and our need for them remind us of our humanity,

a cosmic joke on us, so we won't forget how rooted we are
to the earth and not the ethereal beings the nuns wanted us
to be. Today I was thinking about shame and I see Dennis,
thin and frail and naked, the skin stretched tight over

his big bones, not an ounce of fat to cover him, the skin blue
and translucent as he crawls from the bedroom on his
helpless legs to the bathroom. How ashamed he is,
as though this illness were a failure of his own manhood

and he to blame, how he pounds his fists on the floor in
frustration, how he scuttles into the bathroom and closes
the door but not before I see the dark well of sorrow in his eyes.
Today when I am thinking about shame, and wish

it were only toilet paper or a red splotch on my dress
or my inability to learn the Periodic Table in Chemistry
that made me feel it, instead of my convoluted feelings
about my husband's illness, how nothing in our lives
is all one thing or another, not love, not grief, not anger,
but always mixed with its opposite emotion. I see Dennis
crawling along the floor, and I am struck with the axe of grief,
a terrible pity that can do no good, but mixed in with it,

the shame of my own impatience when he can't
remember something I told him two minutes ago
or when he struggles for twenty minutes to open a package
and won't accept help, or when he insists he can walk

down the stairs and falls, the corrosive shame of my quick
annoyance, the shame of my lack of patience,
the shame of feeling that his illness is a deep
and muddy river in which we both will drown.

Obviously, I didn't really want to present this negative picture of myself in my poem. As I was writing this poem, I found myself crying, but I forced myself to keep on writing it. I knew it was something I needed to say and that, many times, when I reach the cave in my own center, I do end up crying. This poem also was one I had great difficulty reading in public; in fact, the first time I read it to an audience I cried. I've learned now that, if I'm going to read a poem to an audience for the first time, and it's a poem that made me cry as I wrote it, I should read it to groups of friends first before trying to read it to an audience.

Sometimes when I'm leading a workshop, I will look up from my own writing (I always write when my students write), and I see that one of my students is crying. The joke in my workshops is that you should always bring a box of tissues with you to class. Going to the cave can be very tough, but it is those poems that cause others to react in a deep, emotional way. Sometimes students begin to cry as they read their poems. I always try to get them to finish reading, even if they are crying, because the next time they read the poems aloud, it will be easier. I guess, it also says something to me about courage—if you can force yourself to get through reading a poem that is from a place so deep inside you that you cry.

Before my book, *All That Lies Between Us*, was published, a friend came to me and told me that the poems about my husband's Early Onset Parkinson's Disease were very moving, but that I shouldn't publish them because it would be a betrayal of him. I worried about it, and then I showed the poems to Dennis and asked how he felt about them and about my publishing them. He said: "You wrote them because you needed to write them, and they might help someone else in our situation so you need to publish them."

Anytime you're writing a poem that deals with long-term illness or disability, you may worry about hurting someone's feelings. However, I think you shouldn't censor what you write. Once it is down on paper, you can decide not to publish the poem in a book or a magazine or you can put the poem away for later publication. You should not try to control what you write and when. I always have the feeling that if you do, you end up killing off the creative spirit in yourself.

Chapter 19

Getting to the Heart

Too much poetry today is made up of beautiful language, exquisite images, polished and sophisticated lines, but it lacks one basic quality – heart. I call it poetry for cowards. I call it sausage poetry, poetry that is interchangeable and cranked out of MFA programs across the country. It is totally recognizable for what it is – a product to be marketed. It is poetry that wears deodorant and is guaranteed not to offend. It is poetry guaranteed to get the writer acceptance in academic circles.

This poetry reminds me of an art exhibit I arranged many years ago. The artist was self-taught and built beautiful sculptures from metal and junkyard finds. Out of copper piping and scrap metal, he built a Model T Ford. It was an exact replica of a Ford, built to size; it had a motor, a battery, a key, a perfectly detailed hood. The students at the Passaic County Community College, where the exhibit was held, couldn't stay away from that car sculpture. It was so detailed, so perfect, so shiny and bright; it's only flaw was that it didn't actually move. The motor was a model of a motor; the key did not actually turn and the battery did not work. It was so attractive, but it did not move.

These sausage poems are like that. They are missing essential vitality; they are missing blood and heart. The poet hides behind the scrim of language, afraid of anything that will reveal the underside of his or her life. These are poets who sneer at hearing another poem about a grandfather; they use the word "confessional" as a way to put down personal poetry.

I heard recently about a young poet who stopped writing for years, because she was told her poetry was too passionate. This professor was encouraging her to write bloodless poems, and he did her years of harm before she was willing to shut his voice out of her head.

I say that only poetry willing to take a risk will last. This book is intended to encourage that first draft of poem, the one where the vitality and heart is found. You can go back and polish the language, shape the lines, add details, but unless the heart is in the first draft, it isn't going to be in the final draft either. This poem "Nighties" from *All That Lies Between Us* is one that went through many revisions, yet I worked very hard to try to retain its vitality.

Nighties

At my bridal shower, someone gave me
a pink see-through nightgown and pink satin
slippers with slender heels and feathers.
The gown had feathers on it, too.

I've always hated my legs and even then,
when I was still thin and in good shape,
I didn't want to wear that nightgown
or slippers, didn't want to parade

in front of you like some pin-up.
But I wore them anyway, all those negligées
I got as shower presents, sleazy nylon
I didn't know was tacky. When I wore

shorty nightgowns, I'd leap into bed
not wanting you to notice how
the nightgown revealed what I thought
my biggest flaw. In all the young years

of our marriage, I wore a different nightgown
every night, not that it ever stayed on for long,
and afterwards I'd pull it back on, afraid
our children would find me naked in our bed.

I felt so sophisticated in those nightgowns,
like the ones Doris Day wore in movies.
Only years later, when my daughter buys me
a nightgown made of soft and smooth blue silk,

do I realize that the first ones I owned
were cheap imitations of this, the one
I hold now to my cheek, grateful
to have been once what I was.

How lucky I am to have loved you
in nylon, silk, my own incredible skin.

Chapter 20

Writing Poetry to Save Your Life

When my life starts to overwhelm me, I recall the advice the poet Ruth Stone once gave her daughter in such a moment: "Don't cry, honey. Write about it. You'll make a million dollars." For me, "writing about it" has never made me a million dollars, but it has helped to save my life. I find that when I can shape my experiences and memories into a poem, even the most painful become bearable. In essence, they lose the power to harm me. By taking experience and shaping it, you, too, will be able to turn what is negative in your life into art, an art that not only illuminates your own experience, but also connects that experience to that of other people.

Claiming pain, and the words in which to express it, is a form of power. As a child who was shy and inarticulate, I had great difficulty speaking up in a group or to any authority figure, but in writing, I became powerful. I found a way to empower myself by using written language to make my life present to others. By writing, and later publishing my work and reading it out loud to groups, I was able to gain increasing confidence that what I had to say could move people. I discovered that, while I was unassuming in person, I could feel my presence growing once I started to read my poems. People came up to me after my readings; they wanted to share their lives with me. They wrote me letters about my poems and books. As a result, my confidence grew.

Claiming my own voice did not come easily at first. Growing up as I did in a working class Italian American community as the child of immigrants, I did not speak English until I went to school. I often felt my outsiderness was as visible as a huge scar on my face. But books and writing made me stand out from the people who inhabited my world. By loving literature and writing and by publishing my work, I was suddenly visible among people who did not have the education or the language to describe their own lives, so other people were defining their lives for them. I soon understood that, if I did not learn how to tell my own story, other people would tell it for me.

Tell your own story. Without books and writing, my life would have been dramatically different from what it turned out to be. I believe that you can transform your life by telling your own story. You just need the courage to begin. *Believe that you have a story worth telling.*

Seize your power.

Chapter 21

The Block Method of Unblocking Writer's Block

I mean this title literally and figuratively. Too often, the critic inside us, our own personal crow, can keep us from writing. *Writing Poetry to Save Your Life* is intended to give you an ongoing method of inspiring yourself to reach into the cave of the past and memory, to find there the stories you need to tell and that we need to hear.

As you continue working, you need to be certain you are carrying your courage and your willingness to take risks. You have to promise yourself and me that you won't listen to that crow that will make you doubt yourself and your purpose.

Because I want you to write every day, I've provided many prompts in the following pages, and I am repeating for emphasis what I've written in previous chapters.

Take out a pen and a journal, notebook or pad of paper. Pick a spot that is quiet and a time when you won't be interrupted, and give yourself the gift of 20 minutes just for you and your writing. Look only at the first block of prompts. Read all five prompts and then choose one. Do not think too much about it. Pick the one that appeals to you the most. Write as though you are speaking directly to the reader. Do not erase or revise as you go along. Write out the prompt in your own handwriting at the top of the page.

Then let yourself go. Write whatever comes into your mind. Let connections form. Do not allow the crow to tell you that what you are writing isn't any good and that no one would want to read it. Let yourself move back in time to the moment you are writing about.

Envision the person you are describing, the place. Call all of your senses into play. Let that inner poet, that person buried deep inside you, write the poem for you. Don't stop until your 20 minutes are up. Use a timer if you need it.

When you've finished, read the poem aloud to yourself. Before you start to read, you will have to knock the crow off your shoulder, because the crow will try to tell you what you've written is terrible and a waste of space. The crow will tell you it's so bad, it's embarrassing. Don't listen. Here is my gift to you – my voice in your head, saying: *Believe in what you've written. The story you have to tell is important and valuable and I want to hear it.*

If you have a friend you trust enough, read this rough draft to that person. As you're reading the poem aloud to yourself or to someone else, you might spot some place in the poem where you've repeated yourself unnecessarily or where the sound of a line seems wrong. Put a question mark next to that line. Put the poem away for at least a week. Only after that much time has elapsed should you even consider revising. You must be careful at this stage not to let the crow ruin the poem by cutting away its vitality and energy.

A poem can take a year or two to revise or it can sometimes be almost perfect after one or two revisions. Each poem is different.

Remember, too, that all of us who have written for a long time have hundreds of poems that don't work. Those poems I keep in my very thick "failed poems" file. It's okay. Maybe I'll go back later and see if there's anything to be done with those poems. When I wrote those poems, I needed to write them, but something about them didn't have the impact I wanted so I placed them in that file. It's okay to have a file like that. Not every poem is intended to be a finished product, but each poem you write helps you to explore your interior life and assists you in making other poems stronger.

On your next writing day, you will move on to the second block of prompts and repeat this pattern, and keep going until you've gone through every block of prompts in this book. Then, go back to the beginning and start again.

The idea here is to surprise your subconscious mind into letting go of its secrets. What does a particular prompt remind you of?

What person does it make you think of? These prompts offer you the magic carpet that will take you to the cave inside yourself. It's dark in there and scary, but that's where your poems and stories are. Take a risk and go inside.

Chapter 22

Prompts to Keep Your Writing Flowing

In the following pages are prompts designed to help you keep writing. They are not prescriptive but meant to jumpstart your creative process. Use these prompts as opening lines or topics. They are put into sections of five, so as not to overwhelm you. Look at a section and pick one that inspires you most.

———⊂══⊃———

I'm always afraid of _____ showing up at my doorstep.

Write a poem about a wedding you went to or didn't go to.

Growing up on my street, in my town, meant …

Write a poem about background noises.

The worst test I ever took …

———⊂══⊃———

My mother's stories …

I am the daughter/father/aunt/son who …

I come from a long line of …

What I told the cops/what really happened …

The most peaceful place I've ever been …

This anger will last.

"Ma, hear me now, tell me your story, again and again" (from a poem by Nellie Wong).

I'm waiting …

I love/hate the phone/internet because …

Teacher you remember … (describe the classroom the way you remember it).

God made it cold in here.

Is there anything in the world sadder than …

Write a poem about big or greased hair.

My mother would never talk about death.

Don't tell me how to …

Write a poem addressed to a poet or to poets in general.

Write about a particular food or drink that you associate with feeling warm and safe.

Write a poem about words or actions you would take back if you could.

Write a poem about a man/woman who left you, or whom you left.

I was never young with you.

My brother / father / husband / daughter is the one who…

Because my alarm clock didn't go off …

Write a poem about your favorite shoes.

Ever since _____ I can't stand the sound or smell of …

Write a poem about ugly people.

I'd forgotten until now …

Reading to the children …

The time I lost my son or daughter …

Your ambitions when you were seven years old …

Write a poem about a particular car.

I think about death …

Answer this question in a poem: Can this really be my life?

The china in my mother's / grandmother's cupboard …

Write a poem of apology.

What did you collect as a child? Write a poem about what you collected or being a collector.

If only I had realized …

Answer this question in a poem: Where do the dead go?

We had seen it on TV and thought we'd try it.

Long, long before I had escaped from a life where …

Write a poem about hats, shoes, or gloves.

When my mother / father tried to tell me about sex / about what to do with my life / about what was wrong with me, they said …

Bringing in wood …

"always and everywhere / go after that which is lost" (from a poem by Carolyn Forché).

The black sheep of the family …

Memory of a day in church from your childhood.

Why are you grieving?

What they don't teach you.

Write a poem about the topic of mortal sins.

I'm fifteen and every day after school I go to …

Donald Rumsfeld confesses in a mosque in Harlem …

What is it inside that is always missing.

Use the word "after" or "because" as the first word of the first line and repeat it throughout the poem.

Being loud enough to wake the dead …

"I'm the only one who has a weird family" (Flip Wilson from Good Times).

"The truth is such a rare thing. It is delightful to tell it" (from a poem by Emily Dickinson)

Write a poem about light.

If I were on a reality TV show, I'd be sure to …

As an athlete …

Write about a personal (perhaps obsessive) routine.

What to call joy and grief.

When I can't sleep, I …

You said …

What I'd most like to leave behind …

How my life has changed …

Write about a time when you were silent and didn't want to be.

Men/women don't usually …

Answer this question in a poem: America, what is happening?

We've lived too long in the shadow.

The food I liked most when I was a kid …

I lost my self-esteem.

Write a poem about your favorite place (for example, a library, kitchen, camp, baseball field, etc.).

I am God.

One shoe in the road …

Laundry on a line …

Write about a picture from when you were a child.

Think of someone whose story you want to tell, perhaps someone who could not tell their story.

In my worst/best dream …

Playing doctor …

When I was a kid I loved to order _____ from the back of cereal boxes.

Why I love / hate the accordion / guitar / piano / Bach / Beethoven / hip hop / country music / rock …

If only I could …

Open your heart and let me see what I've missed.

Answer this question in a poem: Who are we when a face opens to us?

On Saturdays we …

Write a poem about something you wanted to say but didn't and now it's too late.

I am here in the Pathmark (or some other supermarket) among the cheeses.

"We have come to this simplicity from afar." (from a poem by Sonia Sanchez)

Write a poem about empathy.

On the night of the funeral / wake ...

When I am empty ...

I've never told you this, but I remember ...

I am / am not a great believer in luck ...

Something I lost that I never found ...

What I know of violence ...

I'm jealous of ... (or) The one thing I'm jealous of ...

Even though girls/boys are supposed to ...

Write a poem about spin the bottle ...

My mother/father said ...

All I really want is ...

Write about some antique or artifact from your parent's childhood.

Write a poem about your cousins.

When I leave you ...

What am I most ashamed of ...

Write a poem about a miracle you or somebody you know experienced.

The last date I remember …

I am my father / mother …

What trees / dogs / cats know …

Write a poem in praise of ectomorph / endomorph / mesomorph

I miss …

Best day of the week …

Write a poem about something you built.

I admit it now …

Write a poem about blame.

Answer this question in a poem: Who are the people in our lives who live only in photographs?

Write a poem using the phrase "This is the hour …" repetitively.

The last time I went to church …

All those years and miles …

Write a poem about a moment when you felt lost.

We got as close to perfect as …

That timeless, seedy dive in …

When I was growing up, my favorite …

Write a poem about daughters: my mother's daughters; my mother as a daughter; the daughter or son I might have had or might still have.

Back in the days when …

Baking with my mother …

Write about some books that were important to you when you were young.

Leaning on the post office counter this is what she said:

I practice selective memory.

Write a poem that is a riff on praying or learning how to pray, or "I've forgotten how to pray."

All the stuff we don't say because it isn't polite …

Write a poem that tries to define America or talks to America.

Going to a bar to look for someone to love …

When the door slammed …

Because it fails us …

This really happened …

Perfect circles …

With every step you take, there is an army of women watching over you.

Write a poem about a cardboard box.

Write a poem about your first room.

Write about your first car or a car that was very important to you or that you loved.

Liars …

Answer this question in a poem: How many ghosts walk in one kitchen?

Write a poem about a bookstore.

Being a family man …

In a particular [time, place, year]…

Answer this question in a poem: Who needs words anyhow?

Write a poem on some American icon, or legendary, pop, or historical figure.

In my house no one needed to say I was a disgrace / perfect.

On entering the driveway of _____, I …

I wanted to take you / him / her …

I am part of it now …

You know you have a weird family when …

Answer this question in a poem: Who are the people inside me whose voices I hear in my head?

She took the money because …

Write about some object or antique from your parents' childhood.

Write a poem about that which eludes us, what we can never hold.

How quickly / early …

Where in the world will I find …

Is there anything in the world sadder than …

I am a monkey.

My neighbors …

In my family we always said …

"In July, that ring of heat we all jumped through" (from a poem by Gary Soto).

Write a poem about eyes.

I can't talk about _____ without crying.

In high school, I had it …

Whenever I hear that song …

The things I can't change …

Write a poem about what needs to be forgiven, who needs forgiveness.

Write a poem about an address.

It's hard to have a sense of humor in …

Write a poem about silence

Think of a fairy tale you heard as a child – Snow White, Rapunzel – and fit it into your life now or imagine what that fairy tale character would have felt if she were living now.

Next time I fly …

The scent of you tells me I am home.

What happens when they finally see me … / Will they ever see me …

I always wanted to be the kind of girl/boy who …

Answer this question in a poem: If we forgive our fathers, what's left?

Although I pretend to _____, I actually …

"And I remember Saturday afternoon at our house" (from a poem by Sonia Sanchez)

When I was growing up my heroes were …

Write a poem about what you would erase from your memory …

Write a poem about your room.

If you were an animal …

It was like being there.

Write a poem about your first college sweetheart.

I am drunk on …

Something about a passport …

I didn't expect to fall in love.

Write about someone who is waiting or not waiting for you.

When my car broke down …

I think about them when I think of you.

For years I lived in …

Write a poem about violence.

Write a poem about visiting the cemetery.

Why we don't express grief.

I was sure if I had _____ my life would change.

Think of an article of clothing that belonged to you or to someone very close to you when you were young. What does it make you feel? Write a poem from that.

On the first day of school …

Write a poem about songs that remind you of junior high.

My neighborhood didn't have any color.

The first horse I ever saw …

Think of something someone said to you and start out agreeing with it. Then turn it around on the person. Like: "You don't look like a poet."

Again, last night, I am running.

Answer this question in a poem: Whose people are you?

All those years and miles.

Waiting at the bus stop …

Write a poem about a person whose name you would like to shut out.

First time I tasted beer / champagne …

People I love the best …

I used to think nothing could be more …

When I can't sleep, I worry …

I am sad when …

Writing in the dark …

In the school lunchroom.

Write about a memory of embarrassment.

Sleeping in a strange bed …

The men I've loved …

A name I always wanted … / The name I was called …

For hours today I watched …

The girls with perfect teeth …

What first comes to mind when you think of the word cheap? Think about all the meanings of the word cheap. How does the word apply to you and/or to events or specific people in your past? What connotations does it have when people apply the word cheap to an article of clothing? With whom or what do you associate cheap shoes or clothes?

No matter how far …

Write a poem about an article of clothing or piece of jewelry that's very important to you: your mother's ring, an old sweatshirt, a poncho from 1969, a pair of jeans, etc.

This isn't high school anymore …

Something about cashmere …

Eighth grade parties …

After the party …

We don't go on dates anymore …

Write a poem that tells the best and the worst about something.

Confronting the mail box …

Write a poem about a memory of someone who has died and frame it in a present day event that triggers the memory.

Answer this question in a poem: What do people sing in their cars?

In a world where nothing is lost …

"We work even as we _____" (from a poem by T.H. Wallace).

I never thought I'd write a poem about …

We've been told so many things over the years ...

I can open ... / I can make ... / or I can teach ...

End of the semester ...

How it is ...

"No one ever told me grief and fear are the same." (from C.S. Lewis)

Answer this question in a poem: How do I say I love you?

My father's name ...

We had no way to tell each other ...

The perfect woman / man

Oh, what are the wages of mercy?

From my mother / teacher / grandfather I learned ...

Write four to six couplets connected by an associative leap. Break the thread every second line and let the emotional momentum carry it across the gap.

I lost my shoes when ...

I am my mother / father / brother when I ...

Write about a childhood memory, one that will remain the same for you and won't ever change.

If superman / superwoman (or whatever hero) was my significant other ...

Write a poem about family vacation.

My ancestors are ...

She had so many versions of the truth.

At seventeen I thought I knew everything.

Write about a moment in your life that seems funny in retrospect, but did not seem so funny when it was happening.

I always wanted to be a contestant on ...

Taking my child to the school bus ...

What I don't feel ...

The men / women in our family were ...

Write a poem about sidewalks.

Write a poem in which you address an earlier version of yourself. Pretend you are speaking directly to that person. Describe what you were like, what you felt, what you wanted.

Write about a disastrous kitchen incident.

Everybody had their family vacation in _____, but our family ...

Even after all these years, I remember ...

My grandfather's mandolin / car / truck / books / cigars / money ...

Write a poem about French kissing ...

Write a poem in which you address a person with whom you have a long history – mother, father, sister, brother, grandmother. Pretend that you are speaking directly to this person, say everything you would like to say but can't. Make us see the person, where is she, her clothes, jewelry, etc.

Since I made up my mind to ...

The silence between us ...

If things were different ...

What will become of this poem ...

Next time …

I didn't see that then …

This is the one thing that scares me …

I wanted to scream …

I am waiting …

Write about something you adopted, not necessarily an animal, maybe a style, a way of life, a persona, or façade.

Write a poem about a time when you stole something from someone.

If I could have my way, I would …

See what happens when …

The poverty here is not in these trees.

I would have, but …

Secrets of a magazine cover girl …

I'm always trying to please.

I am standing in the back of the school gymnasium …

What if she never meant to …

Grandma (or someone else) held my hand like …

Answer this question in a poem: What is the road that leads you here?

Banking the fires …

Write a poem / prose poem / prose piece about a photograph you wish you had taken but never did.

I don't let people know …

I have never been …

Write a poem about a childhood photo that you particularly remember.

Because one is always leaving …

When I go to a department store at Christmas …

My father was a young man then.

Describe your childhood room. What was your favorite thing about it?

We are the women / men who have suffered alone.

On the first day of my life …

It's a bedroom …

Describe your kitchen by choosing an object in that room and writing from the point of view of that object, and extend it into a simile or metaphor.

Write a poem about potatoes.

Love is …

When your mother / father dies / moves in with you …

Think of a fairy tale you heard or read as a child: Snow White, Rapunzel, Princess and the Pea, Beauty and the Beast, Hansel and Gretel, Sleeping Beauty, Three Bears, Three Little Pigs, and imagine that you could make that fairy tale character speak. What would the character say?

Every day in the life of man / woman is a …

Sunday morning at our house …

Write a poem about TV shows you always wanted to be a part of …

Tell a family secret.

What shall I pack in my box marked spring or summer?

"Lord, what fools these mortals be" (from Shakespeare's A Midsummer Night's Dream).

How can any girl know ...

Answer this question in a poem: How do you learn to live with the past?

When my car was new ...

So much that is broken or lost ...

Reading a story to my child ...

Dinners of my childhood.

Answer this question in a poem: What do I know how to do?

I guess it's about time someone kissed in this family.

Write about bruises.

Write about what it means to be a girl / boy / man / woman, and how you learned that concept.

"We are his people" (from T.H. Wallace).

That time, years ago, driving west ...

Write about a birthday you remember best.

We started dying when ...

My father's / mother's voice ...

I woke up in someone else's ...

Answer this question in a poem: What is it I don't want to know?

Answer this question in a poem: If you had a big bag stuffed with regrets, which regret would be heaviest of all?

Write about a moment in the past when you disappointed your mother or father or grandparent or someone who served in that capacity.

If I were a superhero …

Learning how to dance …

No room for myself in a house full of …

I didn't know love would hurt this much.

Sometimes I think I'll never …

The way I sleep …

Write about going to the funeral.

Write about Sunday mornings.

First day of a new job …

My mother was the only one I knew who …

What I think when I …

Write a poem about that girl or guy friend who was your substitute/backup/reserve relationship to your primary romantic entanglement.

Write a poem about your ancestors that looks at them as a way of understanding yourself. You could start with an object that was passed on to you or a quality you have that you inherited from your ancestors. What would you like to pass on to your own children?

What is this absence in the heart?

Write a poem about identifying (or not identifying) with your name's ancestry.

I don't know her by name …

Write a poem in which you speak in the voice of a character from history or literature.

I've grown to appreciate insanity.

The things I cannot throw away …

Think of some song from the past, some half heard melody that repeats.

In our house we always …

The woman / man I loved when I was …

Write a portrait poem of a member of your family, or of yourself, your town or city, the place where you grew up, your street. Make use of smell, sounds, the kinds of things a particular person would say, what kind of clothes the person wore. Where do you imagine the person to be – in a kitchen, office, barcalounger, walking out the door?

The time I cut my hair short / let it grow / dyed it / streaked it …

"A sleeping child gives the impression of a traveler in a far country" (from Emerson's journals).

It just grew there …

As we go from shop to shop …

Now that a month has passed since you left me …

Write about something under your bed: dogs, dust balls, a present …

"Don't tell your brother" (from a poem by R. Guido DeVries).

On a Greyhound bus …

I am afraid …

Visiting _____ in the hospital …

At twelve, I thought …

The gift I never got …

Write a poem about something that makes you angry.

Write a poem about something you wanted when you were a child and didn't get.

Write a poem about your first girlfriend / boyfriend.

Write a poem for your father, saying all the things you have never said.

I am lonely when …

Four o'clock makes me want to kill …

I'm scared of …

Write a political poem about something happening in the country where you live right now.

Running away …

Write a poem about plumbing.

Write a poem about riding in your parents' car when you were young. What are the smells, sounds, sights?

Now that you are dead and gone …

I feel lost when …

Sitting in the driveway …

Write a poem about your first vacation.

Write a memory poem using these words: slap, belt, hide, sorrow, mother, sting, jump, dance.

Write a poem about throwing up.

Write about shame. What is it that makes you feel ashamed? When was the first time that someone or something that happened made you feel ashamed? Go back to that time in your mind. Try to recreate the scene. Where was it? What did the place look/feel/smell like? Is there a particular person or action that you associate with shame? In what context was the word used when you were growing up?

When I was eleven, I lived ...

Write a poem about America.

What ever happened to ...

Even at 12 I knew how easily we break.

The safe place I keep searching for ...

This is the street you have walked down ...

Write a poem that has in it: a banging window, yellow linoleum, an unmade bed, a plastic bag.

Riding on the school bus ...

Answer this question in a poem: Can anything save the earth?

My bones cry out ...

My first pair of ...

I was sure he / she was looking at me ...

Write about an object from nature.

Green / blue is ...

Answer this question in a poem: Why is it so hard to tell the truth about our lives?

Every member of the family ...

When I was growing up, our house smelled like …

Write about something someone told you about yourself that comes back to haunt you.

Write a poem about waving goodbye.

If I were a man / woman I would …

Describe a job you have or had. What the place looks like, etc.

"This is the land that time forgot."

So many things are forbidden / taboo for me.

My mother always called me in early for dinner.

Write a poem about a phone number – forgetting it, remembering it.

Write a poem about a doll.

Write a poem about cheap shoes.

The first time I saw my father I was …

The hardest thing I've ever had to do …

Everything is political.

Gary Soto wrote: "At ten I wanted fame …" What did you want at that age?

Carpe diem.

My favorite circus performer …

How to make pesto …

Write about a place that you remember from the past and that you associate with one person – either yourself at an earlier age, or someone else – and write about what it was like to be in that place either in reality or in your imagination.

If I had to stop talking, the last thing I would tell you is …

Write a poem about lines, or people in lines.

What Superman / Wonder woman / etc. meant to me …

What we expected / What we didn't get …

When I saw my reflection …

Listening to that music I hear …

Experience is what you get when you're wishing for something else.

Write a poem about where drunk men go.

Write a poem about the way you dressed twenty years ago, or how you dress now.

Write about climbing trees.

Making small talk.

Mom, she says, you'd hate him.

Why my mother dressed in the closet …

Rain on the roof …

My mother always let me …

Write a poem about drought.

The first time I realized I was different …

Write a poem about building something.

Our lives are in danger …

I'd like to get out of my body …

These few hours of solitude …

In our house nobody ever …

Describe your room as a child or your mother's room. What does it make you feel?

When I woke up calling my mother's name …

There's so much noise in …

The date from hell …

Sitting in the hospital waiting room …

What is it about you that makes me so angry?

From my mother / father I learned …

Why I want to strangle my mechanic …

In the art gallery …

The hardest thing she ever had to do …

I walk the dark street.

Inside me there is a child / old woman / old man …

If I could get someone to come to your class / house, which poet or writer would it be, and what would you ask him or her?

Flattery will get you / me anywhere / nowhere …

I have driven country roads / highways.

Answer this question in a poem: How do I pack up the house of my life?

I haven't suffered enough …

What I want for you...

"I never liked long walks" (from Jane Eyre).

The last time I ...

How it is ...

My mother's mother (father's father) was ...

In my dreams I hold you.

Will I ever stop missing ...

The ghosts that inhabit your life ...

Write a poem about a sixteenth birthday party.

My body is the ultimate mystery.

The ritual of morning ...

Write a list poem of people I've hurt; my failures; cars I've had; people I've loved; places I've lived; movies / foods I love, etc.

At the shore/lake/mountains/on the boardwalk where I ...

The first picture I remember when I think of you.

Write a poem about a train, plane, or bus you've missed or almost missed.

In the car on the way, we ...

Answer this question in a poem: What do you need to visit the dead?

Death is a path we take to meet on the other side.

Before I left ...

Our family has never been one to talk things out.

What I hope to remember about my father always …

Write about bearing witness to something.

Write a poem about cleaning house.

I remember the day I left you …

Gargoyles remind me of …

Write about iridescence. What does the word iridescence mean to you? When have you felt iridescent? Have you met someone or had a particular experience that seems iridescent to you? Was there a particular time in your life that seemed iridescent?

Write a poem about Sundays.

When I return to …

Finally, I enjoy my mother.

I was born at …

My bellybutton …

My mother's talent was …

Shall I bear witness to the nameless child who can't stop …

Now, after all these years I remember: the conversation, the classroom, the dinner, the kitchen …

Growing up poor / rich / middle class / Jewish / Protestant …

Write a poem about the morning news.

Write a poem about your opinion about something.

Write a poem about your favorite color eyes.

Write a poem about thirst / hunger / need.

I'm looking for you (mother/ grandfather) in all the old …

Write a poem about stairs, up or down.

If I could sing a duet with anyone it would be …

What I want …

It was a long winter …

If things were different …

I will die in _____ on a _____ day …

Why should I be surprised?

Write a poem about the sweetest or meanest thing anyone ever said to you.

Write about your most embarrassing moment.

I like it hot.

All the things we cannot learn to say.

The worst haircut I ever had …

In my desk drawer …

Gary Soto wrote: "It was a sad time for the heart." Write about a time like this.

Talking about underwear.

I approach writing like I approach skydiving.

Even when he was there, he was missing.

When I was growing up, I …

A freshly paved street …

The first time I left home …

How they met …

On a daughter leaving home …

Things that are missing …

In my hometown, we …

My body is …

My mother / father never …

Where I came from …

The last time …

The faces I make / The faces I wear …

Tell me …

I have many pictures to choose from …

Sooner or later we face the dark.

Write a poem about your parents' wedding day.

Write a poem about Sesame Street.

Write about Lent, or sacrifice, or something you've given up in your life.

I told you …

All the self-help books are in the bedroom.

What my parents do not yet know …

The man / woman I hooked up with last night.

Think of someone from your past who bullied, made fun of, or mistreated you in some way and write about that person. Speak directly to that person.

Write a poem about waiting for someone to say a particular thing: I love you; you're ok; you look beautiful; you did a good job; I really admire you.

Why I hate taking charge, following orders, standing in line, waiting, etc.

Write about a prom you didn't go to / wished you hadn't gone to.

"When I come to where our house was" (from a Gary Soto poem).

The heat of his / her hand.

Write about your most boring job.

The house on _____ street where I grew up.

I / We can talk about these things because it's different now.

In many families telling family secrets is taboo, a kind of betrayal of the people inside the family group. Telling stories, however, is acceptable, particularly if they reflect well on the family and even if they don't and are humorous. Think about the secrets you weren't supposed to tell and write a poem that tells them or tell a story about someone in your family or a story that was handed down in your family.

The first time you kissed …

Last will and testament …

My best friend …

Answer this question in a poem: Who are these people who live only in photographs?

My mother's / father's / sister's idea of a fancy meal ...

Write about the past and / or future.

Look, the fifties / sixties weren't anything like that ...

Answer this question in a poem: What used to be in the empty Styrofoam cup on the street?

My father won't talk.

My family makes me feel ...

Write about a piece of jewelry or clothing.

Write about clothes / accessories / rhinestones / glitter.

Cleaning out the closet.

I used to wish I ...

Write the story of where you live: mountains, ocean, stream, plants ...

My mother / father always wore her / his perfume / sandals / jewelry / black suit on / to ...

Wearing my mother's / father's clothes or shoes ...

Write a poem about your seventh grade classroom.

Because you died, I never ...

When I was little and someone ...

Answer one of these questions (or all) in a poem: What do I save? / What do I worry about? / What do I need?

Write about a time when you didn't have a chance to say goodbye or said goodbye to a lover.

The story of my life / day …

Sometimes I pretend …

When I am sleeping I am …

I worry about …

Clenching my teeth …

I never liked my name / a particular song / book.

Article passed down by a family member …

Answer this question in a poem: How often have I tried to please you?

It can't happen …

What once was …

Write about cell phones.

Write about the first house in which you lived.

When I look at an ocean, pond, river, lake …

What can't I face about someone I love …

Losing my nerve is / isn't like losing my wallet …

Write about fury.

The house I live in …

If I was in a band it would sound like …

Even in the family photo, you're the one who stands out.

Write about your first dance.

If I could speak to the dead, I would …

No one wanted to dance with …

I wonder where you are tonight.

Write about a time you felt invisible.

Looking out a window …

Write about the person who disliked me / I disliked the most when I was a kid.

The best movie I ever saw as a kid was …

The last thing I say …

Write about a moment from personal history suddenly remembered.

Write a poem in which you draw a portrait in words of someone who is very important to you.

What are the words you now, or always, wanted to hear spoken?

Man / woman / father / mother / child I loved …

Sometimes I forget how fragile the heart is.

What other absences will I have to learn to welcome?

His voice brought me here.

Those were the days …

Go look in your drawer and write about what you'd like to throw away but can't.

Write a poem on biblical characters.

I don't know how it happened …

Write about a friend or some unlikely person from childhood who made a lasting impression.

We were / weren't a Brady Bunch family (or some TV family) …

The other day I spotted Elvis Presley in Wegman's.

If I had the nerve, I'd tell my brother / sister / cousin / aunt / mother …

Sometimes I wonder what happened to …

On the class field trip …

If I asked, would you …

I'm thinking of the dress I wore when …

If love were like an animal, what animal would it be?

This bed … / My first bed … / A bed I remember …

Write about something that happened in the past that made you laugh or cry.

Some things need to be said out loud.

I am in love with …

Write about getting out of bed.

Write a poem that includes a date forty or fifty years ago, a song, a Tibetan monk, a mahogany highboy, a pink Cadillac.

Boyfriends are not like husbands …

Walking through the graveyard …

Even though he/she _____, I …

Answer this question in a poem: Do you know what it is to hate somebody for leaving when you need to have him / her there?

Write about parties.

Women write to women authors; men write to men authors.

He was almost always silent.

She is her mother's daughter ... / He is his father's son ...

What I remember first when I think of you ...

I imagine the stairway in the house on ...

Write about learning the two-step.

Write about glasses.

If only ...

The things we tried to say ...

When I can't sleep I worry about ...

Describe your street.

What I remember best.

"The man who loved to call me stupid" (from a poem by Cornelius Eady).

My bad habits ...

What is the biggest lie you ever told and why did you tell it?

Write a poem about a celebrity.

The last / only time I stole something.

Write about a cab ride.

If only I could change / bring you back / love you / stop loving you.

We don't laugh / we don't smile.

My father was a young man then …

Only in America …

Write about the world as seen by a particular animal.

Early autumn song …

My mother asked me …

I see a young girl / woman …

I told everyone …

Now close your eyes and tell me …

Things I love and things I hate …

Write about money.

Write about the Fourth of July.

The dead are always with you.

Write a self-portrait.

Like many men / women before me …

Write about something you feel remorseful or sad about that you didn't do.

Write an elegy to what is gone in your life.

Write about a time when you failed or seemed a fool.

The words I didn't say …

What I did when I cut class …

I remember when I had my ears pierced / my hair cut / I rode a two wheeler / my brother left for college / overnight camp.

Write a poem that repeats "If…" at the start of each stanza.

"All your biography preserved in your face" (from Sonia Sanchez).

"My mother read everything except books" (from Tobias Wolff).

Write about a particular person from grammar or high school. What you would say to him or her if you could?

In the fifth grade there was a girl / boy who used to …

Loss is …

Write about a time when someone left / moved away / died / broke up with you.

The men / women in our family were …

Who do I remember?

In my secret mind …

Write about forgetting someone's name.

In the lingerie aisle at Victoria's Secret …

In seventh grade, my favorite song was …

Write about a moment after someone misunderstood what you wanted and gave you the wrong thing.

Why I never …

Adolescence …

The baggage I carry …

Answer this question in a poem: Do you feel like a man / woman yet?

My father had both his parents in our house, the TV was always on.

Write about a particular holiday.

Write about names/ nicknames.

Write a poem about a song that brings back memories of a particular time.

The night we hit a deer …

She / He said it was my fault.

If I could wake up anywhere I choose …

Because my mother …

Beauty is …

Write about your mother or father at the age you are now.

I know someone else would have figured it out sooner, but …

It's easy to get trapped in our own history.

What have you done for me lately?

If there is one relative I'd pretend not to know, it would be …

Write a poem about river(s).

My favorite song reminds me of …

If I could start over …

Comfort food …

In the movies no one ever ages.

The last time I had to visit a government office …

It's kind of like fishing / hunting / swimming / diving.

When I am naked …

All the girls or boys I've kissed …

Even the things I did well got on her nerves.

My best friend …

I always wanted to write about … / I can't write about … / how can I write about …

Mr. Clean…

Write about your favorite piece of furniture.

Answer this question in a poem: What was hidden in your house?

My mother was always angry / violent / loving / upset / lost …

Cinderella's glass slippers …

It was not meant to be this way …

What my mother said …

Mom / Dad forgot to tell me …

Ignoring someone on purpose.

Write about being caught.

How I learned to dance …

My brother is …

Write about fists.

Write about your mother's mother.

Write about yourself as seen by a particular friend, relative, lover.

The distance bleeding between us …

You seem so confident / shy/ aggressive.

What our names do ...

After school ...

Write an elegy to someone.

Think of someone who is dead whom you wish you had met. Describe the person. Imagine hanging out and talking to her / him.

Answer this question in a poem: What blooms in winter?

The choice is never clear.

Write about going to the dentist or the doctor.

The rooms of my childhood are full of ...

When pink turns to lavender / lavender turns to green ...

Write about being afraid to care too much for fear the other person doesn't care at all.

Getting dressed in the dark ...

High tide ...

The party I didn't go to ...

Answer this question in a poem: Are we ever satisfied?

If I could take three things out of my pocket / purse / wallet they would be ...

I took a deep breath before I rang the bell ...

Write about seeing a particular movie.

Listening to that music, I hear ...

Write a poem in the form of a letter.

Write about a particular meal that you remember: When was it? What food was served? What was said? What wasn't said? What did you feel? What were people feeling in the room?

A stranger in my house …

Here is something once lost …

Write about a teacher you loved or hated.

Write about a particular day or year or time in your life that was important to you.

In my family we didn't …

Because of my father's job …

You never sit still.

Write about a movie that you associate with yourself or growing up or a particular movie theater.

"I walk through the rooms of memory" (from Marge Piercy).

My kids scare me.

A moment when you wanted to get away but couldn't or didn't.

Answer this question in a poem: Where does it come from, this hunger?

Growing up in my mother's house.

Other folks have better luck.

Write about Nancy Drew / Black Stallion / Bobbsey Twins books.

Out my window …

Feeling green …

Growing up [Italian, Jewish American, or _____] …

Karaoke night at the bar and grill.

"Your face is a doorway that slams closed in the dark" (from Ruth Stone).

Write about family dinner.

Answer this question in a poem: How do you speak to the dead?

What I did was listen.

Write about particular clothes, tastes, styles, etc. you inherited from the dead.

When I had the chicken pox …

Write a list poem: take one room and make a list of 20 things in that room. Cross out ten. Make two poems – one is a list and the other an expanded line for each item.

Winter stays.

What am I ashamed or afraid to tell?

Going to a bar looking for someone to love.

Start with a line of dialogue that has stayed with you and then describe the place and time when you heard it.

I am fourteen …

Write about the words you've always wanted to hear spoken.

Write about your most vivid memory of my childhood.

If you have to go, I suppose that's the way to do it.

If he / she had loved me …

Answer this question in a poem: What can we do to save the earth?

What it takes to survive.

I was old enough to know ...

Write about particular memories associated with a book.

What keeps / kept a family together?

Each year, they arrive.

We used to have things we believed in, names for all the things that were larger than we were, more beautiful ...

Enjoying my Mexican breakfast ...

No one will say why ...

It was in 1964 / 1974 that I first ...

There was a time when ...

The first time I ever kissed a boy or girl ...

Answer this question in a poem: Who are the ghosts who haunt our house?

How nature saves us.

Write about the ways people walk.

The time I was most frightened in my life ...

Write about your first sexual experience.

When I left my house ...

The smell of friends ...

Some of us never really leave high school.

Would you have loved me more or less?

Alone in the woods …

Write about rewriting the past.

Write about a street, neighborhood, town, and the person with whom you associate that place.

Write about a personal event that appears unexplainable.

If I had another chance …

The attic in our house …

Write about that which cannot be said.

Write about something that made you ashamed or triumphant or terrified.

_____ was my boyfriend / girlfriend in first grade.

What I don't feel …

Flip to a random word and write a poem about it.

Write about one of the following: people you have hurt / loved; cars you've had; places you lived; movies you love.

Your arms are a deprivation chamber.

Let it pass you by.

My worst job / boss / paper / teacher / friend …

Again!

In the basement, the damp places of life …

Low cut jeans …

A day in the country …

How things change.

The loneliness of growing up …

Write about a moment in your classroom when you felt your students were laughing at you, or when you were a child and other children laughed at you.

That was the day I'll never forget.

Watching the river rise …

Her name was _____ and it suited her.

Feed someone you know.

In the stacks …

Write about Sunday outings with my family.

Write an ode about some small thing (like your socks).

Wearing my mother's clothes …

This is not my name.

My father is a quiet ghost / a talkative ghost / a rambunctious ghost.

The missing father …

Answer this question in a poem: Why do you never say what you mean?

I want to write a poem about love / peace / war.

Write about growing pains.

Green Buddhas …

Write about what you didn't learn in school.

That New Year's Eve I didn't …

Show me the way out.

Sometimes I feel like a hot fudge sundae / baked potato / Buddha / courtesan. Why? Try for an extended metaphor.

All the while I've been shopping in …

Write about a Halloween costume.

Drinking to blot you out, I …

"I never understood the girls who had the sweater or the latest hairdo copied out of a magazine." (from D. Wakowski)

Language difficulties …

I never told anyone about …

Write about a word or phrase that you associate with a particular time, place or person from your past.

Write about curtains.

Write about something you did or didn't do with your father.

She smokes in the girl's bathroom.

Ode to my uterus.

My first real poem was about you / it / that time.

I knew my life had changed when …

What was it about that house?

She/he might have been my friend but …

Something I can't forgive myself for …

Ourselves or nothing …

I'm still angry because when my parents didn't _____, I felt …

This is the poem in which I finally tell you …

In my house there are no …

If I asked, would you …

Reading him/her to sleep …

Write about a teacher or a moment in school that you particularly remember.

If you do what you've always done, you'll get what you always got.

I wish you'd understand.

Write about firsts: your first date, first kiss, first day of school or college, first child, first time you won or lost something, first love, first time you left home.

When I was eight I thought …

I really didn't enjoy …

Blowing a fuse …

What blankets are for …

All along I've wanted …

Digging a grave …

What I like / love / need …

My mother's bureau …

Your hands are …

Write a poem honoring a teacher.

I remember the concert when …

Write about what it is like to turn 20, 30, 40, 50, etc.

"Remember this" (from a poem by Lucille Clifton).

These are the words you have said over and over.

Write a poem on the first day of school: yours, your child's, a teacher's.

How to make a mess …

We used to call it downtown, remember?

The day he / she died …

What we love in the corners of our lives …

First thing I remember …

First time you drank too much …

Write about chicken pox.

I don't know when I started …

Last time …

When my alarm rings …

Write an ode to any body part.

How sad I am today, how lonely.

A bright improbable pink …

The last time I heard Led Zeppelin, I …

I didn't find out my father was in jail until …

Answer this question in a poem: How long should I mourn?

What scares me …

This poem is …

Things my mother didn't tell me …

Joy at the center of things.

In 19__ sex was … or … When I was thirteen, sex was a …

When I loved you …

She is the one with eyes …

Write a poem that has a five word title, a street name in your town, and a piece of living room furniture.

Our house was always open / closed.

If I could change one thing about my looks …

Write an environmental poem.

Who are the women who …?

Write about someone you had a crush on.

Write about swimming in the harbor at red tide.

I get cold now …

My father ran the streets.

Sticky kisses …

I am practicing letting go …

What is your sacred place?

There was this boy / girl who used to …

Write about doing something with my son / daughter / mother / father: fixing steps, baking a cake, sewing a dress, arguing …

In the newspaper today I read / saw …

The lost photograph …

If it weren't too late, I'd …

I was a faithful watcher of …

If I lived in New York …

Start with a poem you love so much you feel you could have written it yourself.

Why are you so …

Write about the worst experience you've ever had in a car.

My crazy aunt / uncle always told me …

Reoccupying the site of injury …

Pick a particular person you remember from the past. What would you say to him / her if you could?

Answer this question in a poem: What remains unspoken between us?

How can any boy know …

I admit it, I was taken in by the ads for …

Write a poem about trust.

The hippie merchants on 4th Ave …

Write about a high school dance.

Write about your favorite color.

Bugs Bunny gets a _____.

My mother / father was …

Smell of obedience …

The nails left in the walls.

Write something about slippers: your grandmother's, your own old ones, your father's, your own sexy or unsexy slippers.

Write about a word or phrase that you associate with a particular time, place or person from your past.

Tell a lie in a poem and at the end admit what the lie is.

Marilyn Monroe, Audrey Hepburn, Julia Roberts, Brad Pitt, Jack Nicholson – any other actor. Write a poem in which you address that person. Tell them about your life. Don't be afraid to be funny.

My father tells me this was once a nice part of town.

In the dressing room mirror …

"My clothes have failed me" (Gary Soto).

My normal life; my ordinary life …

Write a poem in which you look at your hand. Really look at it and then describe it in detail. What moment does it remind you of? Weave in and out between the hand and your life.

November music …

Write a resume of your life and turn it into a poem.

When a room becomes lonely …

This is the last poem …

Write a poem about a disaster that happened to someone else.

Write a poem about a friend you liked but your family didn't, or a relative your family liked but you didn't.

The article of clothing that …

Because you've never said …

I always wanted to wear support stockings / girdle / white gloves / a cross / a locket / high heels.

For the first time my family went …

I had thought the choices would be clearer …

Write about heritage.

The basement …

Write a poem about the same scene / object / building in a different season / weather / time.

Write about hysterical laughter.

Write about something you were afraid of as a child that stays with you now.

My father always wore …

Write a poem that uses these words: crocodile, ocean, dragonfly, skitter, erupt, fiery, discombobulated.

I want …

Write about guilt.

I never watch TV in the mornings.

Write about a moment when you wanted to get away but couldn't or didn't.

Everyone complains about …

My first pair of grown-up shoes …

You know what I don't like about this room.

On nights I stay home alone …

My mother calls to warn me …

I'll save what I can.

My father always drove …

There are a lot of ways to die.

The taste of his / her skin.

I am not my father / mother …

I have two left feet.

Sitting in Dunkin' Donuts or Friendly's …

Write about alcohol.

I have a reputation for being …

Write about a seashore memory; a funhouse memory; a roller coaster, boardwalk, zoo, or circus memory.

Sadness roots in everything that breathes.

For no good reason …

I'm ten, and every day after school, I …

In my grandmother's / mother's kitchen, or some holiday meal, or a memorable meal.

Write an imagistic landscape poem – an urban or natural landscape, a place you've been, the physicality of it, emotional quality of it.

Dinners in our house were …

In my body, it is winter, it is spring.

My first bicycle / doll / toy …

Neighbors who pretend not to know ...

The family pet really belonged to ...

I know everybody in _____, but I never ...

Write about the first time you remember lying to yourself.

Write a portrait poem.

In high school we ...

Write about parking.

Imagine your mother as a girl, your father as a boy. Write about that.

Write about the words you have always wanted to hear spoken.

Write about keys.

In the attic ...

Maybe all there is, is the next thing that happens.

Ten long seconds ...

Walking my dog ...

The last time I lost my mind ...

Write a eulogy for something or someone who hasn't died.

My father took me ...

It's strange that love and grief turn out to be the same thing.

I hate to admit that I watch ...

Write about middle school dances.

The thing I like about oatmeal …

Write about favorite boots / shoes / coat / hat.

It is blank as hell …

I'm ashamed of myself.

I wish I could be …

First time I left home …

What you need to do …

You look better in the dark.

Use the word "after" to begin each line: after the party / after graduation / after work / after my first child / after the first year of my marriage / after I got my degree / after I got angry.

Write a poem that starts with a quote from someone in your life, something the person always says to you.

Ars poetica (a piece on the art and nature of poetry).

I am beautiful / lonely / sad when …

The first thing I ever saved my money for and bought for myself …

Looking at the constellations …

Write about anguish.

When I wake up at 3 am …

The world is so noisy.

First time I saw my mother or father cry …

Write about Valentine's Day in grammar school.

If I could change one part of my personality …

My first real poem was about you ...

In my dreams I fly ...

Write about doctors.

I want to dance.

My mother is reading ...

Write about early morning.

The women in your family have never lost touch with one another.

Swimming in the harbor at red tide.

My student / co-worker / guy or girl in my apartment building who looks like my ex.

Grief is ...

Bad and all the ramifications of the word: When was the first time someone called you bad? Define bad as it relates to your experience of the word. What does the word make you feel? How has the meaning of the word changed for you as you've grown older? Write a poem called "Bad."

In twenty years I'll ...

Who was the odd kid you remember from school? Were you the odd kid? How did that kid make you feel then, and when you think about him or her now?

What's that smell?

Never again ...

Mom, Dad – couldn't it have been different?

When I went to the zoo, I identified with ...

In the movie *The Graduate* there's a scene in which the character
is standing in front of a fish tank watching fish swimming around in
circles. Think about this image in relation to yourself, your life or to the
world, and let it take you wherever it will.

Describe building or making something, and learning how to do it.

Pick a year, a particular grade and write about it.

Love is a long shadow, a dark …

Because I did not die …

I found her / him again this morning.

My last piggyback ride …

Write about getting stuck physically or emotionally.

So that I wouldn't sleep, I …

I never intended …

Answer this question in a poem: What else can I ask for?

The names I've called myself …

Things I could or could not do; things my brother / sister could / could
not do …

The dead walk among us, unable …

Write about winners / losers.

Write about a crash.

Write about war stories.

When my _____ tells me …

This winter …

The silver heart, the crystal beads.

In Atlanta / Boston / Denver (or another city) …

Answer this question in a poem: How do we connect to the world?

What's missing?

Write about a liar.

At sixteen, I worked …

Where I lived when I was a kid …

Write a poem that uses quotes from somebody from your past to build a portrait of the person.

Answer this question in a poem: What brings us out?

I have to _____ before anything else I love gets away.

Remembering you …

Write about leaving a message or the unreturned phone call.

The photo on the milk carton …

Write a poem about your home state.

I imagine St. Francis or St. Jude speaking to me.

Something I have forgotten …

Something I still don't understand …

Write about love, hope, fury, injustice, rage without ever mentioning those words.

Answer this question in a poem: What is it we can't forgive in ourselves?

Listen …

Suppose …

Answer this question in a poem: If the moon could speak, what would it say?

We all wear the scarf of regret.

Answer this question in a poem: What can you do with a book?

When the jukebox or band played.

Tonight, I am …

Write about listening to the Grateful Dead.

Write about learning how to make do.

Write about the song I love best, the song that reminds me, the song that always makes me cry.

Some lessons you never forget.

What I remember about that day …

Write about red Jell-O.

Write about legs.

My mother gave …

Write about Wonder Woman.

Saving it …

People ask me how I like living in …

I was named after …

Write about having a club.

After ...

Write about Bette Davis eyes.

Write about smoking / blowing smoke rings / KOOL.

Write a list poem: things I love ...

When people ask me, "Did your mother hold you?" I ...

Write about learning how to ride a bike.

When I look in the mirror I see ...

When am I most alone?

Barbie falls out of love.

I am ...

Write about writer's block.

Poem in praise of ...

Hour of the snake, hour of the wolf, hour of the fox ...

We were still girls / boys then ...

Answer this question in a poem: How do we outlast despair?

What we once thought was ugly ...

What do we bring with us, what do we take away?

Riding the Ferris Wheel ...

I still think no one loves me.

This winter could kill me ...

In my remembered childhood, it is always …

If only I'd …

How to begin again …

It is your face I think of when I remember …

Everything happens so fast.

The morning after …

Missing you …

Where are they gone?

I don't care that …

Move closer to me.

Show & tell.

My father worked late.

Write about your first bicycle.

Answer this question in a poem: Why are people so afraid of being touched?

Plenty of words for hate …

I imagine my mother falling in love.

Home before dark …

Write about a summer job.

It was that way in our family …

My friend tells me …

In my basement ...

My father / mother / grandfather / grandmother spent his / her life ...

The headline this morning ...

Why do you always think you're it?

My horoscope ...

Write about the boardwalk.

Write about a password.

Answer this question in a poem: What can I do about it?

The world is ...

What did I expect?

The town / city where I grew up ...

When I'm, nervous or upset I ...

How fortunate I am to have ...

Write about old-time radio.

The streets of my city / town.

The phone rang ...

_____ makes me scream.

Why I write ...

Write about being soaking wet.

Ode to my underwear ...

Answer this question in a poem: Can we start again?

I want a tattoo of ...

In the Wal-Mart ...

What day is this?

Being the good girl ...

I tortured you all through school.

I know how to live ...

The man standing next to me on line in Wegman's.

Write about a newspaper photo.

Answer this question in a poem: Why I read the obituaries?

Riding a Harley with James Dean.

It has taken me a long time to surface.

I still have my pride.

This is not what we had in mind.

The songs help me remember what it was.

The hard way was the only way you knew.

I never intended ...

Answer this question in a poem: What can I ask for?

Write about winners / losers.

The names I've called myself ...

On Sundays we …

When my _____ tells me ____, I …

The trip of my dreams …

This winter …

Write about something personal that you were doing when some major event in the world was happening.

The silver heart …

The crystal beads …

Write about what makes you angry.

Things I could and could not do …

My people are …

The most unpopular kid in the class …

Double Dutch …

At sixteen, I worked …

Where I lived when I was a kid …

These are my people …

Answer this question in a poem: What is it about morning light?

Answer this question in a poem: Is this the way it is with fathers / mothers?

Because I saw …

Write a love song for a place or a time in your past.

I knew I wouldn't …

At dusk …

On days like this …

My hair …

Write your own story about being different.

Write about your home economics / shop class.

My _____ is like _____.

My _____ is _____.

Write about the inside of your car.

Too bad you're not Catholic, you could call on St. Anthony.

Those Volvo SUV's are so ugly.

What we can't say to ourselves.

I keep losing men / women.

My wife / husband says I'm such a crybaby.

I had a dream about …

Nomadic kisses.

Your mama said …

I must confess …

I want to visit the grave of …

My inner child is throwing a tantrum.

In a chat room with …

Every time you sing that song …

Poetry is the way I want to say something to you.

I'm sorry, I'm hysterical.

By the time this is over I will break …

I'd better not find myself in any of these poems.

Write about Sunday dinner at Grandmother's.

Corn nuts and jelly beans …

It came to you like grace.

Baseball nights …

I just want to go back.

I would have given anything to leave.

Leaving Penn Station / Binghamton / Canal Street …

Write about regret.

What if …

I'm busy being a philanthropist.

I'm busy being …

Don't hold on too tightly.

I'd rather be …

Yes, I am a cheerleader.

I love this long-sleeved shirt.

Every time I write about _____, she / he …

What can we do to save the world?

Don't you ever dare.

The closer you are to …

I got an email about …

It's so hard to let go.

Make a list of short phrases starting with the word don't.

Write about a newspaper photo.

Why I read the obituaries.

So much that is not right in the world.

Why I am poor at …

Some of my worst wounds …

I open my mouth and …

In my grandmother's house …

Dancing the jitterbug / funky chicken …

Why I'm so bad …

Why I love to dance …

Why I could / couldn't climb the rope …

My favorite beauty mark / birthmark …

What nudity is to me …

In 1995 or 1996 I am …

I'll run naked through the streets.

I don't know what to do about …

Write about an eating disorder.

When _____ told me …

What I wish I hadn't done …

The teacher I hated the most …

This spring …

If the truth be told …

I never thought I'd sleep with …

Climbing barbed wire fences …

Write about running away.

I can't help but be hot.

The first time I climbed a tree …

What silence is.

Instead of ____, I eat chocolate.

"I miss who I used to be" (from Jen Simon).

What a haircut can tell you.

The girl / boy I loved in second grade.

When I think of high school, I think of …

The last time I flew a kite ...

Global warming is caused by ...

The only picture I've ever kissed ...

The cologne reminds me of ...

You can't get Chinese food at 3 AM in Binghamton.

Stranded on a desert island with George Bush and Colin Powell ...

I don't have much ...

Reading in New Haven ...

Why I hate instant messaging ...

Why it's impossible to hide ...

If I were in Survivor, I would ...

I think it's time to start drinking.

The chances we take ...

The house at the end of the street ...

I know you remember ...

Write about an avocado-colored shirt / skirt.

I never liked silk.

Rosemary is for remembrance ...

Watching my child sleep ...

All the locks are latched.

What they warned us about …

Answer this question in a poem: What terrifies us?

Write about a second kiss.

In that borrowed dress / car …

When I dream of _____ I wake up ____ …

Simple jobs …

My mother never had much …

What was I thinking when …

Stooping to pick up pennies.

I always take the time.

It's too late for her.

Write a poem on forgiveness or I forgive you.

Skip to My Lou; A-Tisket, A-Tasket, a green and yellow basket…

Write about yellow.

This is where he said …

I hadn't done that until 10th grade.

The gospel according to Eve …

No one calls your name.

Blue like …

Down on _____ street, they …

My daughter says …

They can tell …

I have forgotten your name

Answer this question in a poem: Have you saved my letters?

You ask why.

I want to ask my father …

I was there when it happened.

After / Before …

Write a portrait of a person you love as he or she was twenty, thirty years ago.

Like a finger loves a scar …

I have a dumb prompt …

Write an ode to something you've never read a poem about.

I'm trying to write a poem that's not about sex.

Singing my child to sleep …

Imagine …

What I cannot forgive in myself …

I heard it from …

Answer this question in a poem: What happened then?

On their wedding night …

On CNN …

This is a protest poem.

Witches don't like the ocean.

Write a poem with a joke in it.

Answer this question in a poem: Have you ever laughed and cried at the same time?

Spending the weekend ...

You entrust them to me ...

Write about puzzles / Monopoly / Trivial Pursuit.

Write about card games: Old Maid, Crazy Eights.

When we played the game *Cootie* ...

In a past life you were _____ to my _____.

People assume that ...

Fearing to tread where angels rush in ...

Write about baloney, malarkey, snake oil, doublespeak.

Will I ever recover?

Write a happy / funny poem.

Celebrating joy.

I hate myself when ...

What I don't like about myself ...

Write about something you did that you're ashamed of.

I'm not ashamed of ...

Answer this question in a poem: What would you do for $300?

I love that movie.

What memories you select ...

I know you lied.

I just saw Courtney Love at _____.

When the monsters arrive ...

I really hope ...

This love affair must end.

Why I hate you / me.

Why I hate New England ...

I don't mean to offend you but ...

Somebody else ...

Slowly I turn ...

My clothes ...

Write about the first day of college.

Someday I'll get that right.

The difference between a poem and a rant.

I wrote a poem that made someone run away.

Write a poem that's an extended metaphor.

Write about running home from school.

Write about the matinee.

Write about having a guest at your house.

Even my best friend / husband / wife / mother doesn't know …

Write about earth / gardening / digging / beach / sand.

The trouble with hate.

When _____ drinks too much.

On pay day …

I want, I want, I want, I want …

Write about cheese or chocolates.

He's throwing them at me.

The summer house / place.

Actually, this is about my mother.

My father / mother / husband drove …

Answer this question in a poem: Do you know what it is to love someone as much as you hate them?

I am trying to see my mother / father / grandmother now, but …

The spaces that do not contain …

The face you came to see …

It is not your house.

At fifteen / sixteen / nine, you are desperate.

Write about what has happened to America since September 11, 2001.

Everything matters …

Staring into the dark …

This is how it works.

During dinner, my parents …

Observing the world keeps us honest.

Write about meeting Picasso or Salvador Dali on a street corner in NYC or your own town.

I often take wrong turns.

Answer this question in a poem: Can you believe the luck?

My mother never / always played bingo / gin rummy / mahjong.

What makes me sad.

Answer this question in a poem: When did I stop looking at myself in mirrors?

Seeing my mother in the bath …

My father disappeared often.

I am not ready to take my place among the dead / to let you take your place.

All the brutal years …

Our history is full of …

We are here still in all our various disguises.

Write about walking the dog.

Write about a wedding day.

When winter comes …

Answer this question in a poem: What is in my mother's handbag / my father's briefcase?

In the Grand Union parking lot …

Why I'm not a good kisser.

Maybe they had it right in kindergarten / first grade.

Write a poem in which every fourth line starts with "because I am / because I am not."

The time I waste.

Answer this question in a poem: What do I want?

You bring me back.

How my heart got to be this way.

Write about how to do something: pull an all-nighter, fall in love, build a shed or a boat or a soap box, make a mess, plan a funeral, love, keep a friend, or anything.

If I could have been …

Names they called me …

Her / his / my father / mother promised nothing / everything.

When I come to that quiet place …

Write about Spiderman or some other cartoon hero.

The night the lights went out …

Going dancing / Why I love to dance …

How it begins …

The cars I drive or my father / mother drove …

Write about trouble.

At twilight …

When my father / mother sang …

Each birthday, my mother …

This is how you want it.

We know a lot / we don't remember.

Nothing keeps …

Hard work …

Answer this question in a poem: What is found there?

Answer this question in a poem: What doesn't matter?

Write about caring too much.

Write about first love.

My mother's girdle …

On the benefits of letting sleeping dogs lie …

My hands come down from …

The last time I cried / saw my mother, father, sister, brother cry …

Write a meditation on sex or sexuality.

Answer this question in a poem: In what language do you dream?

Crossing over language …

I expect to find my mother and father in _____.

Impossible nightmares …

Write about sirens.

Answer this question in a poem: What are the words I need to say?

Write about lamplight.

When I first read / saw _____ ...

At 18, I thought ...

Write about the movie theater.

Write about your favorite cereal as a child.

Write about a trip to the 5 & Dime store.

My senior picture or class photo ...

Write about autumn colors.

No matter how old I get, part of me stays sixteen.

I am / am not my mother's daughter.

My father's son ...

Glass shadow ...

The girls and boys in fourth grade ...

Write about your earliest memory.

Write about learning to polka or do the tarantella or the bunny hop or the funky chicken.

Ode to my thumb.

Write a surreal poem.

What does it take to ...?

You can make the story different.

Listen ...

Here is the story I write ...

Try this ...

Write about hair – my mother's, my father's, my own.

Write about paper dolls.

When I first read ...

At the wedding ...

Write about making love.

In the old trunk ...

I fell in love with a man / woman who ...

Movies I went to ...

Write a radio poem.

Frogs, fields, dandelions ...

What I wanted ...

This is mine ...

The day I was born ...

Perfect numbers ...

Everyone has a story. This is mine.

I always wanted to come from a town where ... or I never wanted to come from a town where ...

On a good day, I ...

Why I loved the Life of Reilly or Leave it to Beaver or The Fonz ...

Answer this question in a poem: What is gone?

Write about gratitude.

My father's hats ...

We named our first cars.

What my father / mother wanted ...

We had so many places we wanted to go.

Because she is a girl / ... because he is a boy ...

Write about learning to build model planes, or to fish, or to cook a roast, or bake a cake, or run a mile.

You've got to play the hand that's dealt you.

Favorite moment of the day or evening.

Answer this question in a poem: What eased down the drawbridge over the unspeakable?

Answer this question in a poem: What love is or jealousy or rage or hate?

Write about a drive–in.

Write a poem about America, a political / angry poem.

Answer this question in a poem: Whose voice is it that I hear?

In our house we were not allowed to talk about ...

Write about taboo.

Answer this question in a poem: How shall I bear witness to the nameless?

Answer this question in a poem: What is sacred?

Write about moving.

My bedroom was painted / I painted my bedroom ...

The bathroom in our house ...

Write a poem about place that focuses on a particular town, street, city, house, that is a microcosm of what America is now.

Write about a movie or TV program that reminds you of a particular time in your life.

Write about what's in your mother's or father's dresser or closet.

Write about learning to ride a bike, drive a car, make a bed, play ball, jump rope.

Answer this question in a poem: What is in the dark at the top of the stairs?

Write about growing up in the 90s.

Write about getting ready for the high school dance.

Answer this question in a poem: What offers comfort?

The rooftops of houses ...

If I had the courage I'd ...

Write a poem defining despair.

Write about how my mother and father met.

I am 13 and ...

I'm not finished with you yet.

The first time I went ...

After all these years, I am going to tell you ...

To my mistakes, or mistakes I have made …

When I think of photographs, the first one I remember is …

The cliches my mother / father / aunt / uncle / _____ lived by.

My 12th birthday …

On TV, the war …

Answer this question in a poem: What has happened?

Write about seeking absolution.

Write a poem about what is happening to the earth.

Answer this question in a poem: What were the songs they played?

Write about TV families you grew up with

Dying alone with a cat …

Never date a writer …

There were no more I love yous.

If_____, then_____.

Answer this question in a poem: What does death carry in its suitcase?

If I had a band …

I'm nothing without what I remember.

Answer this question in a poem: What is unsettled between us?

Write about the onset of puberty.

I'll let you know when I get …

I think I'm turning into a slut.

What I'm afraid to say ...

There are many rooms in the house of poetry ...

My poem would never ...

After work we ...

All morning in the September light ...

I'm afraid of ...

If our hearts had been pure we would have ...

Answer this question in a poem: What opens in the skin of the world?

Someone should take her picture.

It's a hard war to figure out ...

Certainly it is daylight in Iraq right now.

We live so much of our lives alone.

Everything seems combustible.

Answer this question in a poem: Why doesn't somebody do something?

Maple Rock Auto Repair ...

Write about cigarettes.

Names I've forgotten ...

Outside your city / town, the highway ...

The singer on the radio ...

I said goodbye to my father / mother ... or I never said goodbye ...

When I was twelve I wanted / didn't want ...

I can see him / her ...

This is my first time trying to ...

Answer this question in a poem: How does the heart decide what to remember?

To the things / moments that shine ...

In my dream there were ...

I tried to pretend it wasn't there.

I want the details.

Whatever you do is enough.

When I saw her / him last.

You have begun to leave me ...

Write about ceremony.

Write about second-hand clothes.

I never wanted to know what was under the bed.

Twenty years later my sister is still ...

Write about the porch.

Write about staying home from school.

Because you keep turning toward me ...

Answer this question in a poem: Why do we always expect to become someone else?

Noticing the world around you ...

My mother used to say, "Don't ..."

The thin thread of pleasure ...

What I regret ...

You have not changed at all.

Ode to my hands, my tongue, my legs ...

We can't tell ...

Write about hiding.

Even when I forget you, I go on looking for you.

Pretend ...

For the first time my family went ...

My first pair of ...

If I were a superhero ...

I approach writing like I approach skydiving.

Although I don't usually admit it, I am a closet fan of ...

Although I pretend to – I actually ...

When I was growing up, our house smelled like ...

On Saturdays, we ...

The first time I realized I was different ...

The worst test I ever took, had ...

Sitting in the hospital waiting room ...

The time in my life I was most frightened ...

I'm still angry that ...

When my parents didn't _____ I felt ...

Song for a long winter ...

How easily we break.

The most embarrassing moment in my life ...

The black cat crosses the road in front of my car.

Someone should take her picture.

It's a hard war to figure out.

We live so much of our lives alone.

Answer this question in a poem: How do we reach into the shadows of the past?

"The world is a burning house" (from the Buddha).

I tried to pretend it wasn't there ...

When I saw her / him last ...

Answer this question in a poem: What defines us?

Pretend ...

To my mistakes ... or mistakes I have made ...

What I believe in ...

More than anything my father / mother hated ...

Watching my father / mother eat lunch …

The happiest day you remember …

You do not want to be here.

We are sorry to inform you …

Things people told you turned out to be true …

Write about a Girl / Boy Scout trip.

On that day, nothing / something happened …

You'd think when things change, there'd be …

This is how memory works …

Suck it up …

I discovered sex / love …

I don't know what it is I mourn the most …

Write a scene in a diner.

No room for yourself in a house full of …

When I speak sometimes I hear my mother's voice.

Answer this question in a poem: What is green, what grows?

Kitchen table stories …

How to live in this world …

Write about your grandmother's sacred recipe.

I could choose to keep …

Write about the cool kid in second grade.

Answer this question in a poem: What is it that my heart wants?

My father / mother always wore …

Because of my father's job …

In my room …

At ten I loved …

Answer this question in a poem: Who will help me find the way out?

When I don't like myself …

Write about your favorite relative.

Why I always loved / hated my sister …

Look around you …

Write an ode to your body.

Write a poem on the subject of beauty, glamour, hair, make-up, body image, fashion, sex symbols, or beauty icons.

Write a poem about a place – make us really see and smell it.

Answer this question in a poem: Who was it I loved that night?

Write a poem about food.

Full house …

What I need …

The places we call home …

Answer this question in a poem: What is it that my heart wants?

How to live in the world ...

Jesus is always appearing in New Jersey.

Write about things you're grateful for.

Write about days when nothing happens.

Make me fall in love with you.

Tell me what it's like to ...

When I turned to look ...

Write about the quiet in this place.

Think about sex ...

I love these Saturdays ...

Now is not the time to question.

The dance of the street.

Write about working the night shift.

My father's / mother's hats ...

I give testimony.

Rain on an empty street, grace ...

When you kiss me ...

Some of us say ...

I typed my name into an internet search engine.

Answer this question in a poem: What is the color of sleep / death / love?

Write about waiting at the bus stop.

Answer this question in a poem: Is there no mercy?

One thing that can save ...

Answer this question in a poem: Does every choice involve losing something?

Answer this question in a poem: What I would do for love?

At home, it's autumn ...

I wait for a sign.

Who would have thought love would ...

I am afraid of ...

What I found in books, music, TV programs ...

It reminds me of ...

Why I grind my teeth in my sleep ...

You never know what you have until you lose it.

When I became a pessimist ...

It had always seemed so certain.

Answer this question in a poem: What were you waiting for?

Write about the Saturday matinee.

Write about a family outing.

All my life I've been waiting for them to come back ...

Write about the summer when ...

Why is it so difficult to lose; what we didn't know about losing …

Write a prayer.

Write a poem with a famous writer in it.

Teach me the science of desire.

The problem with my name …

The problem with my sister / brother …

If you're a girl, a boy, say 14 years old, living in …

Answer this question in a poem: What sadness / loneliness drove him?

When I was a child, I thought …

Every year in my town we always …

The past is an …

Every Christmas / Hanukkah, we …

My family is …

I promised myself …

Write about your first best friend, or why you didn't have any best friends.

The grammar school teacher I remember.

"Everything that rises must converge" (from Flannery O'Connor).

Write a poem to a female poet.

Write a poem about the internet.

Adversity, perseverance, redemption, miracle …

Running away …

You never know …

When a man loves a woman / when a woman loves a man …

Write about something lost in translation.

The big storm …

The coldest winter …

My poem would / would never…

After work we …

You imagine your mother as a girl / father as a boy …

You don't know much.

I imagine my mother falling in love …

We lived on the edge …

Plenty of words for hate …

The jobs I've had …

When I got mugged, my mother / father …

At the drive-in …

We are almost home …

Answer this question in a poem: America what is happening?

Blessing the house …

I was the girl who / boy who …

Answer this question in a poem: What was she thinking?

I was in love with …

Write about trying to keep a secret.

Answer this question in a poem: What do my hands reach for?

We / Our parents used to play cards …

For years now, my father …

Just yesterday …

Standing on a train platform …

I am trying to remember the girls / boys I used to love.

I made a fool of myself.

Write about desire.

I'm making a list of …

My parents never stayed in motels or went out to eat.

When my father / mother sang …

When I am invisible …

I no longer recognize myself.

Write about a February morning.

Write a poem about studying biology [or other science].

Answer this question in a poem: What makes the world tilt?

Answer this question in a poem: What do I love about the past?

Answer this question in a poem: What is there to praise?

In the Wal-Mart sporting goods aisle, two women / men ...

So many people fall away / are left behind ...

The present I gave my third / fourth / fifth grade teacher ...

I imagine my mother dancing ...

We all need our own order.

That summer we learned ...

Write about family love / hate.

On the record ...

Write about a guessing game.

Answer this question in a poem: What is it that I don't want to know?

Write about a moving day.

Answer this question in a poem: Why is it so hard to decide?

If I could be born again, I would want ...

Things I've grown to love / can't forget ...

The first time I understood what it means to be lonely ...

Answer this question in a poem: What color would I like to paint the world?

Answer this question in a poem: What landscape is the landscape I claim as my own?

Write a poem about a turnip or a sweet potato.

When my father / mother was young ...

Write about bathing by candlelight.

What do I know of my father's father, or my mother's mother?

When we had music …

I would not confess …

Write about the first day of high school.

Write about what you never had the chance to tell someone or your mother / father never had the chance to say.

Answer this question in a poem: Do you know what it is to need what you don't have?

I worked there every day after school.

Ode to the ordinary, the everyday.

My father / mother showed me how …

We used to sunbathe, our skin …

What can't last …

What endures …

Write about the street you lived on.

Anything goes in …

Everyone's off someplace warm …

Write a poem that includes the names of songs or a singer you love or loved.

Things like this happen …

Some nights are easy.

The cramped geography of my life.

Lucky are those who …

I catch myself whispering please …

Choose a word or phrase – forgive me, because, save me. Write a poem that uses them repetitively.

It's almost spring.

What is the color of love / loneliness / loss …

Sometimes panic overwhelms me.

Of course it didn't last.

Write a portrait of your parents.

The pictures on my living room walls / my mother's mantle …

How to be happy …

What I should have done.

I used to blame my mother / father.

What is not there …

Answer this question in a poem: Have you ever walked through the country of grief?

It was forbidden to touch …

Write about your refrigerator.

On being cool …

The newspapers are full of stories, so many stories I've read lately …

What I notice when I look closely.

Write a poem of praise.

We used to sing along with the radio.

I'm four / five / six years old ...

I'm worried about ...

Things that burn ...

Poets love the stuff by the side of the road.

On spring nights, we drove ...

She knows what it's called ...

At recess, we ...

The people who come after us.

I was never into the kinky stuff.

Holding on ...

Answer this question in a poem: What are the habits of our hearts?

Again my bed is empty ...

Write about what you do when you can't sleep.

The first time I saw ...

Tell me again how ...

In my restless memory, how lovely it was ...

In the memory of their faces.

Letters to the dead ...

Write Beatitudes for the Twenty-first Century: Blessed are ...

Write a poem of protest.

Write about using your father's / grandfather's razor or watching your father shave.

There is no language to say …

I wear my grief like …

My thoughts are prayers.

I'm trying to keep something down.

Walking in my town, I've seen …

If my father and I have anything in common …

Write a poem in which you try to imagine your father / mother at the age you are now.

Sometimes you can wish so hard …

Write about sleeping in a strange bed.

It's so complicated, this loving …

I still see them some nights.

I will not surrender to the failures of my body.

Answer this question in a poem: How many games have I played?

Bless the girl / boy who …

The last thing I want to talk about …

Write a poem about the kitchen table.

What is lost or never was.

When I am not sure …

Why is it so hard to decide / to choose …

Write about getting dirty.

Answer this question in a poem: What manner of love is this?

Thinking of Thoreau …

Write about locked doors.

Once I believed it was either the life I wanted, or nothing.

Write about going to bed.

It was that way in our family .

Write a poem in which every line is a quote from someone about things you should do or you should be afraid of. Tell us who said the line.

Answer this question in a poem: Who remembers women ironing?

The first day …

The phone call …

_____ never stops speaking before the answering machine shuts off.

Answer this question in a poem: Where do we find redemption?

Write about the relationships between mothers and daughters or fathers and sons.

Write about eavesdropping.

All that must change.

Write a poem about rebellion.

Why am I afraid.

Answer this question in a poem: What is happening to the world?

Answer this question in a poem: What used to be green?

This is the poem I want to write.

Write about your mother's regret.

I still see him.

My days feel like …

Our house was filled with …

The polar bears are drowning.

In Australia, they are killing stingrays …

Answer this question in a poem: How do I find what I need?

Geese are flying in the wrong direction.

Write about some important moment or event in your life that you connect with something that happened in the world on the same day.

Answer this question in a poem: What place am I rooted to?

Answer this question in a poem: Why do we destroy the very things we love?

Answer this question in a poem: What can we do to heal?

On the way to class …

Write about the tongue.

Answer this question in a poem: Why do I love mangoes?

My father learned to …

Write a portrait poem of someone you know from your neighborhood.

I imagine tracing my finger …

If only I could name what I long for.

Write about superstitions.

What are the colors …

Write a list poem that answers the following question: What I love / hate / need?

Write about eating alone.

All the boys / girls wore them.

I don't know what came first.

War or exile …

Being able to say what I want …

Write about buying new shoes.

We're driving the elephants crazy.

On the news …

When my father / mother came home …

Answer this question in a poem: How do our eyes work?

What I overheard …

What I expected …

I was a camera recording …

Write about passing from shadow into light.

Why I'm a naturalist …

I fall for every woman / man I meet.

Answer this question in a poem: What gets lost? What can be saved?

War and all its ramifications …

Let me tell you …

This is the year I learn …

Write about three people you remember from 7th grade.

That was when I started / stopped smoking.

It was winter. I imagine …

Write about showing off.

Write about a box or urn. What does it hold?

In a box marked the past I find …

Write about a treasure chest.

Answer this question in a poem: What can we do to ward off evil?

I heard my / your heart beating.

I'm putting my faith in reincarnation.

Parking in the graveyard …

Write about the people in your town / America.

Ugly.

I don't know how to tell the story.

Answer this question in a poem: What watches us?

We don't deserve it.

Write about day trips.

Answer this question in a poem: What makes me sad?

I believe in ...

I am mourning.

What I saw ...

Bedroom song.

Write about hanging curtains.

While driving my car, I am thinking ...

Write about a moving day.

Answer this question in a poem: What do I notice when I look at the world outside?

Each of us has a name.

What would I ask for on the final ...?

On a day like this ...

If I am the wolf ...

We believed ...

Write about the place where you bought your first CD / record / cassette tape.

Write about the wall between the present and the future.

From my father / mother I learned ...

Write about everyday dangers.

Answer this question in a poem: Why I went /didn't go to summer camp?

If my grandfather could tell the story of his life, my grandmother …

"The history of whales is a history of serial disasters" (from Greenpeace).

Answer this question in a poem: Where do I want to go when I die?

This is the way the world comes back.

Now that I have …

This poem is for …

Answer this question in a poem: What do we honor, what do we celebrate?

Write about going to the shoe store as a kid.

There are landscapes we cannot control.

The dead sit calmly among us.

Write about learning to be grateful.

In Chin's restaurant …

Use the word "unknown" as the first word of every stanza or line.

Now, in November …

Sometimes I can't sleep because …

Answer this question in a poem: What happened on my front porch?

We took what was given.

Write about bullies, what bullies have said / say.

Why I / my brother / sister / father / mother love(s) video games.

Your mother's sisters, your father's brothers.

Write about pretty girls or a pretty girl.

Answer this question in a poem: What remains?

In my dreams …

What the teacher said …

Answer this question in a poem: What do we leave behind?

My dead father's hand …

Write a poem in which you repeat "If you …" as the start of stanzas or lines.

By day you can bear almost anything.

Write a poem to rivers, streams.

It's not right …

What can we do to atone?

I let the spirits in …

We share the world …

Think about the most embarrassing moment of your life and combine that with something you read about in a newspaper or saw on TV. Go back and forth between the two things.

Write portrait poems of your sister or brother or a cousin.

Write about speaking across generations.

Before something happens …

You promised …

Write about the sixth grade.

Stick to your own kind.

I've always been afraid of ...

Accidents can / do happen ...

Write about hats: your mother's winter hat, grandpa's hat, the hat I wore to, the hat my father wore to ...

One more year alive ...

What is the sorrow that never leaves, the space inside me nothing can fill?

Answer this question in a poem: How will one of us live without?

Write about how you learned religion.

Answer this question in a poem: What is that sad road ahead?

Waiting for spring in the endless mountains.

What I know about America ...

Answer this question in a poem: How did we all get tricked into believing in fate?

We live in an age where ...

Write a poem in which you take on the persona of a famous person in politics, music, movies.

When I was ten I watched ...

Oh, what do you want anyway?

The last time I saw ...

Write about X-ray machines, fluoroscope machines, going to the doctor ...

When I open the door, my father / mother ...

Answer one of these questions (or both) in a poem: What escaped us? What we wanted to escape?

In the slow unraveling of love ...

Our breath, our need, our sorrow ...

It is memory that turns ...

So what is this place where love / anger / hate lives.

Write about watching a war on the news.

I want to find my way back.

Tonight in my father's / mother's house ...

Even now, I'm still searching for a thing to keep.

Answer this question in a poem: Is this the way it has to be?

On the way home from school ...

What I believe ...

Answer this question in a poem: What is it like waiting to be kissed?

I now know so much more ...

This afternoon I could almost think nothing's changed.

After recess ...

One perfect thing I / my mother / father can / could do ...

July in my hometown meant ...

Write a poem using the following words: winter, Crackerjacks, Bruce Springsteen, geometry, map.

Write about Cinderella in middle age.

Write about a family party.

It's Saturday night, senior year.

We'd meet at the diner after ...

Write about a movie star or singer who was very important to someone in your life. Include both that person in the poem and the star they loved and why.

What I'm waiting for.

Black ice ...

When I'm feeling sad, I ...

Bullies.

At 14, I told my father / mother ...

Driving through my town ... Let your mind jump around. Make your own connections between lines. Let one thing remind you of something or someone else. Don't censor yourself.

Answer this question in a poem: What steps do we need to forget or remember?

Even I ...

The glaciers are melting in Juneau, Alaska.

Even the bees are vanishing.

Meeting the obscure dead ...

Why is it sometimes loneliness ...

Someday I'm going to re-read Proust / learn to speak Italian.

The boss ...

I want to name all of them, the living and the long dead, before I am, too.

Write about trying to start a garden.

Forgiving …

Answer this question in a poem: Why do we need to destroy everything?

On TV we watch the bridge collapse.

The food that gives me comfort …

Write about something you never expected to do.

Answer this question in a poem: Is this it, after all?

I used to know what it meant …

What I remember most …

Everything comes to an end.

The last time I saw my mother …

Traveling …

That's the way we sleep now.

We must witness …

We bend our memories to fit …

The game I loved …

Answer this question in a poem: How does sadness get caught in our throats?

In Georgia, a lake, almost as large as the sea, is drying up.

Write about survival.

Answer this question in a poem: What is it about 3 am?

We are always trying to return ...

Imagine reading a story to a child (possibly yours) / a sister / brother, or someone reading a story to you. Write a poem about that.

What I wanted to be.

Answer this question in a poem: What would you like to (not) pass on to your children?

All the things I've never let myself say ...

Write a political poem. Connect it to your own life.

Write about something someone told you about yourself that comes back to haunt you.

At 19 or 12 or 8, I did not know ...

In my new school ...

How I lost my best friend ...

Sometimes I get so worried, it's hard to breathe.

Answer this question in a poem: Why do some moments get caught in our memory, the smell of them, the sound?

Saying goodbye ...

The night we broke up ...

Even now, I want ...

What I like about myself; what I hate about myself.

Games I've played ...

Go away. I want to be alone with Dylan Thomas / Rilke / Neruda.

In these green mountains …

The music of the universe is everywhere.

In the silence before sleep …

Write about Christmas morning / a night of Hanukkah.

Write about homeroom in high school or junior high.

I don't remember …

My favorite teacher/grade. The teacher/grade I hated.

What I wrote in my notebook when I was twelve …

Write about family breakfast.

What I long for …

Letting go of the past …

You can't make this stuff up.

How I learned irony.

Write about your mother / grandmother's wedding picture.

The strangest gift I ever received or gave …

Write an ode to your mother's hair.

We were not prepared for it.

Write about the first cigarette you smoked (or didn't).

What is it about you that makes me …

Answer this question in a poem: How far away are the dead?

What I want that I know I can never have …

Write about turning sixteen.

Answer this question in a poem: What did I think would happen?

Write a poem about love or loss or grief or all three.

Write a poem that includes Iraq, George Bush, Joe Torre, a kangaroo, a kid from your high school class.

Missing you is like …

Sometimes I feel I have forgotten how to speak.

The clothes I wore.

Answer this question in a poem: What makes me ashamed?

About The Author

Maria Mazziotti Gillan is a recipient of the Barnes & Noble Writers for Writers Award from *Poets & Writers*, and the American Book Award for her book, *All That Lies Between Us* (Guernica Editions). Her latest book is *The Place I Call Home* (NYQ Books). Her webpage is www.mariagillan.com.

She is the Director of the Creative Writing Program/The Binghamton Center for Writers, and a Professor of Poetry at Binghamton University-State University of New York. In addition, she received the Chancellor's Award for Excellence in Scholarship and Creative Activities from Binghamton University.

Maria is the Founder and the Executive Director of the Poetry Center at Passaic County Community College in Paterson, NJ, and editor of the *Paterson Literary Review*. She has published fifteen books of poetry, including *The Weather of Old Seasons* (Cross-Cultural Communications), *Where I Come From, Things My Mother Told Me, Italian Women in Black Dresses,* and *What We Pass On: Collected Poems 1980-2009* (all by Guernica Editions). She is co-editor with her daughter Jennifer of four anthologies: *Unsettling America, Identity Lessons,* and *Growing Up Ethnic in America* (Penguin/Putnam) and *Italian-American Writers on New Jersey* (Rutgers). Her work has appeared in *Prairie Schooner, New Letters, The New York Times, Paddlefish, Connecticut River Review, Poetry Ireland, Connecticut Review, The Los Angeles Review, The Christian Science Monitor, LIPS,* and *Rattle,* as well as in numerous other journals and anthologies.

Maria has won the 2008 Sheila Motton Award, Primo Nazionale Belmoro, the First Annual John Fante and Pietro di Donato Award, the Aniello Lauri Award, the May Sarton Award, the

Fearing Houghton Award, New Jersey State Council on the Arts Fellowships in Poetry, and the American Literary Translators Association Award through a grant from the National Endowment for the Arts. She has also received the New Jersey Governor's Award for Literary Outreach and The Dare to Imagine Award from Very Special Arts.

Her poems have been read by Garrison Keillor on The Writer's Almanac. She has been interviewed and has read her poems on National Public Radio's (NPR) "All Things Considered," "The Brian Lehrer Show," "The Poet and the Poem," "The Leonard Lopate Show," as well as "In honor of National Poetry Month," "The Charles Osgood Show" on CBS-Radio, also on Pacifica Radio, and Voice of America. She has also been featured on several PBS-TV (Public Broadcasting System) programs. Her books have been chosen as Editor's Choice by Booklist, New York Public Library Book List, and one of the American Library Association's Outstanding Books for Lifelong Learners. Her poems are included on state and national tests in North Carolina, Tennessee, Minnesota, Texas, and Italy. She has read her poems numerous times at universities, festivals, and poetry centers throughout the USA and in Italy, France, Yugoslavia, Finland, Wales, and Ireland. The Maria Mazziotti Gillan Collection of her papers is housed at the Binghamton University Libraries.

Bibliography

Barkan, Stanley. *ABC of Fruits and Vegetables*. Merrick: Cross Cultural Communications, 2012.

Beatty, Jan. *Red Sugar*. Pittsburgh: University of Pittsburgh Press, 2008.

Boland, Eaven. *In a Time of Violence*. New York: W. W. Norton and Company, Inc., 1994.

Boss, Laura. *Flashlight*. Toronto: Guernica Editions, 2010.

---. *Arms: New and Selected Work*. Toronto: Guernica Editions, 1999.

---. *On the Edge of the Hudson*. Merrick: Cross Cultural-Communications, 1993.

Carey, Kevin. *The One Fifteen to Penn Station*. Fort Lee: CavanKerry Press, 2012.

Cavalieri, Grace. *Water on the Sun*. New York: Bordighera Inc., 2006.

Clifton, Lucille. *The Collected Poems of Lucille Clifton 1965-2010*. Rochester: BOA Editions, Ltd., 2012.

---. *Good Woman: Poems and a Memoir 1969-1980*. Rochester: BOA Editions Ltd., 1987.

---. *Two-Headed Woman*. Amherst: University of Massachusetts, 1980.

Covino, Peter. *Cut Off the Ears of Winter*. Kalamazoo: New Issues, 2005.

Daniels, Jim. *Show and Tell: New and Selected Poems*. Madison: University of Wisconsin Press, 2003.

---. *M-80*. Pittsburgh: University of Pittsburgh Press, 1993.

Derricotte, Toi. *The Undertaker's Daughter*. Pittsburgh: University of Pittsburgh Press, 2011.

Doty, Mark. *Fire to Fire: New and Selected Poems*. New York: HarperCollins, 2008.

---. *Atlantis*. New York: Harper Perennial, 1995.

---. *My Alexandria*. Champaign: University of Illinois Press, 1995.

Duhamel, Denise. *Ka-Ching!* Pittsburgh: University of Pittsburgh, 2009.

---. *Two and Two*. Pittsburgh: University of Pittsburgh Press, 2005.

Geok-Lin Lim, Shirley. *Crossing the Peninsula*. Portsmouth: Heinemann, 1980.

Gillan, Maria. *What We Pass On: New and Selected Poems 1980-2009*. Toronto: Guernica, 2010.

---. *The Place I Call Home*. New York: NYQ Books, 2012.

---. *The Weather of Old Seasons*. Merrick: Cross-Cultural-Communications, 1993.

Gillan, Maria and Jennifer Gillan. *Identity Lessons: Contemporary Writing About Learning To Be American.* New York: Penguin Putnam, 1999.

---. *Unsettling America: An Anthology of Contemporary Multicultural Poetry.* New York: Viking Penguin, 1994.

Ginsberg, Allen. *Howl and Other Poems.* San Francisco: City Lights Booksellers and Publishers, reissued 2001.

---. *Collected Poems 1947-1980.* New York: Harper & Row, 1984.

Gluck, Louise. *Averno.* New York: Farrar, Straus and Giroux, 2006.

Heywood, Leslie. *Lost Arts.* Hammond: Louisiana Literary Press, 2013.

---. *Proving Grounds.* Pasadena: Red Hen Press, 2005.

---. *Natural Selection.* Hammond: Louisiana Literature Press, 2008.

Hillringhouse, Mark. *Between Frames.* Copenhagen: Serving House Books, 2012.

Howe, Marie. *What the Living Do.* New York: W. W. Norton and Company, Inc., 1997.

Kowit, Steve. *The First Noble Truth.* Tampa: University of Tampa Press, 2007

Liebler, M. L. *Wide Awake in Someone Else's Dream* (Made in Michigan Writers). Detroit: Wayne State University Press, 2008.

Liebler, M. L. and Ben Hamper. *Working Words: Punching the Clock and Kicking Out the Jams.* Minneapolis: Coffee House Press, 2010.

Lifshin, Lyn. *Lost in the Fog.* Georgetown: Finishing Line Press, 2008.

---. *Barbaro: Beyond Brokenness.* Huntsville: Texas Review Press, 2009.

McNaugher, Heather. *System of Hideouts.* Charlotte: Main Street Rag, 2012.

Murphy, Erin. *Science of Desire.* Cincinnati: Word Tech Communications, 2004.

Olds, Sharon. *The Father.* New York: Alfred A. Knopf, 1992.

---. *The Gold Cell.* New York: Alfred A. Knopf, 1987.

---. *The Dead & the Living.* New York: Alfred A. Knopf, 1984.

Perry, Penny. *Santa Monica Disposaland Salvage.* Fallbrook: Garden Oak Press, 2012.

Piercy, Marge. *Colors Passing Through Us.* New York: Alfred A. Knopf, 2003.

---. *The Crooked Inheritance.* New York: Alfred A. Knopf, 2006.

Plath, Sylvia. *The Collected Poems.* New York: Harper Perennial, 1981.

Reese, Jim. *Ghost on Third.* New York: NYQ Books, 2010.

---. *These Trespasses.* Omaha: Backwaters Press, 2005, 2006.

Rich, Adrienne. *Diving Into the Wreck: Poems 1971-1972.* New York: W.W. Norton & Company, 1994.

---. *The Fact of a Doorframe. Poems 1950-2001.* New York: W.W. Norton & Company, 2002.

Rodriguez, Jose. *The Shallow End of Sleep.* Sylmar: Tia Chucha, 2011.

Rodriguez, Luis. *Concrete River.* Seattle: Curbstone Press, 1995.

Sanchez, Sonia. *Does Your House Have Lions?* Boston: Beacon Press, 1998.

---. *Homegirls & Handgrenades.* New York: Thunder's Mouth Press, 1997.

Sexton, Anne. *The Complete Poems of Anne Sexton*. Boston: Houghton Mifflin, 1981.

Shipley, Vivian. *All of Your Messages Have Been Erased*. Hammond: Southeastern Louisiana University Press, 2010.

---. *Gleanings: Old Poems, New Poems*. Hammond: Southeastern Louisiana University Press, 2003

---. *When There Is No Shore*. Hammond: Southeastern Louisiana University Press, 2002.

Smith, Patricia. *Blood Dazzler*. Minneapolis: Coffee House Press, 2008;

---. *Teahouse of the Almighty*. Minneapolis: Coffee House Press, 2006.

Soto, Gary. *New and Selected Poems*. San Francisco: Chronicle Books, 1995.

Stafford, William. *Stories That Could Be True: New & Collected Poems*. New York: HarperCollins Publishers, 1977.

Stern, Gerald. *This Time: New and Selected Poems*. W. W. Norton & Company, 1999.

St. Germain, Sheryl. *Let It Be a Dark Roux: New and Selected Poems*. Pittsburgh, Autumn House Press, 2007.

Stone, Ruth. *Second-Hand Coat: Poems New and Selected*. Cambridge: Yellow Moon Press, 1991.

Weaver, Afaa Michael. *The Plum Flower Dance: Poems 1985 to 2005*. Pittsburgh: University of Pittsburgh Press, 2007.

Weil, Joe. *Painting the Christmas Trees*. Huntsville: Texas Review Press, 2008.

---. *What Remains*. La Plume: Night Shade Press, 2008.

---. *The Plumber's Apprentice*. New York: NYQ Books, 2009.

Wolfe, Thomas. *Look Homeward, Angel* (poetic novel). New York: Scribner, 2006.

Williams, William Carlos. *Paterson*, Ninth Edition. New York: New Directions Publishing, 1958.

---. *Pictures from Brueghel and Other Poems*. New York: New Directions Publishing, 1967.